You'll qualify as an AA Driving Instructor

So many companies now offer driving instructor training, why choose the AA?

Well, firstly we're one of Britain's most experienced motoring organisations, with a pedigree of over 100 years.

Secondly, our comprehensive training course covers everything you need to know about becoming not just any driving instructor, but an AA Driving Instructor. This includes 60 hours of face-to-face coaching with an experienced AA trainer who will be assigned to you for the whole of your training.

All our trainers are carefully selected and the training is flexible enough to fit around your existing commitments or condense it if you need to get through the training quickly. At the same time, we train you not just to be good enough to pass, but to become a first class instructor.

When you train with us you are automatically offered an AA franchise once you achieve ADI status and obtain your green badge, the mark of being a fully qualified instructor. Start your franchise within three months of qualifying and we'll discount your fees in your first six months by £1,500 in recognition of having trained with us (subject to terms and conditions).

You will have our full support as you start and grow your new AA franchise business – beginning with a free 2-day induction course, which also includes business and marketing skills training. As you progress, you will be invited to attend our free development workshops and local meetings where you will meet fellow AA Driving Instructors to network with.

To find out more about
AA Driving Instructor Training, call 0800 316 0331
Or to apply for an AA Franchise, call 0800 3 288 288

Driving School   For the road ahead

That's why you'll find starting up with us is reassuring

At the AA we know that starting out on your own as a driving instructor can easily give you a few sleepless nights. After all, you're not just teaching people to drive, but you're also learning to run a business.

However, as an AA Driving Instructor we'll support you all the way to make sure your new career is everything you dreamt it would be. For a start, you will quickly be put at ease by our warm welcome, thorough induction process and the full support of a local AA Instructor coach to see you through your first days.

Naturally, as it is your business, you are in the driving seat in terms of where you want to operate your franchise and the hours you want to work. There is never any pressure from us to take pupils, or to work outside your area or your preferred working times.

The AA franchise fee includes the supply of a striking AA liveried Ford Focus or Ford Fiesta tuition vehicle, which is replaced every 32 weeks, and all running costs except fuel. A replacement car will be delivered within 24 hours (often sooner) in case of an emergency, to provide continuity for your pupils.

Help keep your costs down by sourcing your own pupils or use our optional Pupil Introduction service whenever you choose.

But best of all, you have the comfort of knowing there is always someone to call on for help or advice – no matter how big or small the problem.

To apply for an
AA Driving School Franchise, call 0800 3 288 288
Or for more information on AA Driving Instructor Training, call 0800 316 0331

Driving School

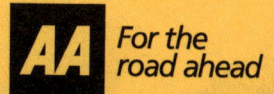

Practical Business Skills for DRIVING INSTRUCTORS

How to set up and run your own driving school

John Miller

LONDON PHILADELPHIA NEW DELHI

Publisher's note
Every possible effort has been made to ensure that the information contained in this book is accurate at the time of going to press, and the publishers and author cannot accept responsibility for any errors or omissions, however caused. No responsibility for loss or damage occasioned to any person acting, or refraining from action, as a result of the material in this publication can be accepted by the editor, the publisher or the author.

First published in Great Britain in 2010 by Kogan Page Limited

Apart from any fair dealing for the purposes of research or private study, or criticism or review, as permitted under the Copyright, Designs and Patents Act 1988, this publication may only be reproduced, stored or transmitted, in any form or by any means, with the prior permission in writing of the publishers, or in the case of reprographic reproduction in accordance with the terms and licences issued by the CLA. Enquiries concerning reproduction outside these terms should be sent to the publishers at the undermentioned address:

Kogan Page Limited
120 Pentonville Road
London N1 9JN
United Kingdom
www.koganpage.com

© John Miller, 2010

The right of John Miller to be identified as the author of this work has been asserted by him in accordance with the Copyright, Designs and Patents Act 1988.

British Library Cataloguing in Publication Data

A CIP record for this book is available from the British Library.

ISBN 978 0 7494 5394 7
E-ISBN 978 0 7494 5841 6

Typeset by Saxon Graphics Ltd, Derby
Printed and bound in Great Britain by MPG Books Ltd, Bodmin, Cornwall

Contents

Introduction	1
1 Becoming an Approved Driving Instructor (ADI)	**7**
What does the job of the driving instructor involve?	9
Training	9
Customers	10
Competition	10
Instructor qualities	11
Benefits	15
Working conditions	16
Franchising	16
Costs	16
Your own driving	17
2 The Approved Driving Instructor qualifications	**27**
The ADI Register	27
The ADI Exams	28
ADI Part 1– theory test and hazard perception	29
ADI part 2 – driving ability	32
ADI Part 3 – Instructional ability	36
Trainee licence	39
The Check Test	40
Instructor training	43
ORDIT	43

Preparation for the exams	44
Training as an ADI	47

3 Working for yourself — 53
Self-employment	55
Strengths and weaknesses	56
Time management	57
Business structure	58
Legal obligations	68
Advantages and disadvantages of self-employment	68
Working as a self-employed instructor	69
Business skills	70

4 Starting up a new business — 75
Business Plan	75
Checklist for start-up	80
Budgets and cash flow	81
Profit and loss projections	85
Loans, grants and finance	88
The driving school car	92

5 Business administration — 100
Using your home as an office	101
Office administration	102
Health and safety matters	106
Value Added Tax (VAT)	108
Insurances	108
Income Tax	112
Tax allowances	116
National Insurance	117
Holidays	118
Pensions	119
Bookkeeping and accountancy	120
Employing other instructors	122

6	**Marketing and promoting your business**	**123**
	Sales and marketing	123
	Customer care and professional standards	131
	Handling complaints	140
	Personal customer service	141
	Code of practice	142
7	**Driving licences and driving tests**	**145**
	Driving licences	145
	Provisional licence	146
	Minimum age for driving	146
	Application forms	147
	Provisional licence entitlement	148
	Riding a motorcycle or moped	148
	Driving licence fees	150
	Vocational licences	151
	Driving Tests	151
	The theory test	151
	The Practical Test	156
8	**L driver training – frequently asked questions**	**162**
	Pre-driver training	162
	Structuring your pupils' training	167
	Pass Plus	176
	What next – after the test	179
	Speed limits	182
	Stopping Distances	184
	Motorways	186
	Drink/driving	187
	Seat belts and child restraints	188
	Accidents	190
	Eco-driving	191
9	**Business opportunities**	**194**
	Pre-driver training	195
	Intensive L driver course	195

Pass Plus	196
Learning materials	200
Minibuses	200
Car and caravan or trailer	201
Fleet driver training	201
Taxi driver assessments	202
LGV training	203
10 Continuing Professional Development	**206**
ADI Associations	209
Advanced Driving Tests	212
Driving instructor qualifications	214
Appendix 1 Useful addresses	217
Appendix 2 Further reading	227
Appendix 3 Information links	230
Index	*232*

Introduction

In the early days of instructor training there were no resource materials or books available for prospective or trainee instructors. When my colleague, Nigel Stacey, and I first started instructor training, back in the early 1980s the Driving Standards Agency (DSA) had not produced the amount of information that is now available. Nigel and I had started organizing instructor training courses on a voluntary basis in conjunction with our own, separate driver training businesses and quickly found that we needed to produce our own training programmes and supporting learning materials for the use of our students. Nigel was running a driving school and instructor training facility in Derbyshire, while I had a driving school in Chichester and a lorry-driving establishment based at Goodwood Motor Circuit in West Sussex.

From those beginnings, *The Driving Instructor's Handbook*, of which I am co-author, gradually emerged – it was not originally intended to be a published book – more a collection of our lesson plans and information sheets about the DSA Approved Driving Instructor (ADI) exams and preparing to become an instructor. Since then the Handbook has evolved into what is now regarded as the 'bible' of the industry.

The Driving Instructor's Handbook now contains up to date and detailed information on all aspects of preparing for the ADI exams: how to qualify as an instructor; what the trainee licence requirements involve; and the regular ongoing check test for all ADIs. The book includes sections on the rules and regulations relating to vehicles, the driver, driving licences and driving tests as well as a chapter on basic mechanical principles. Other subjects that are included involve structuring the learner's training; instructions and terminology; and teaching people who have a disability.

In the early 1990s Margaret Stacey (Nigel's widow and business partner) and I produced *Practical Teaching Skills for Driving Instructors*. This came about as a result of feedback from various people in the industry who felt that there was a need to extend the information into more of the teaching, learning and coaching skills needed to be a successful and effective driver trainer.

Practical Teaching Skills takes the teaching/learning process a stage further, with detail about motivation, how people learn, and the different teaching techniques that are used in L driver training. The book is much more about improving your practical skills as an instructor rather than simply preparing to pass the ADI exams.

For many years now, both *The Driving Instructor's Handbook* and *Practical Teaching Skills for Driving Instructors* have been listed by the Driving Standards Agency (DSA) as essential reading for the Approved Driving Instructor (ADI) exams and have been regularly updated by the authors.

More recently, many new entrants to the industry are now starting up as completely independent, self-employed instructors or franchised by one of the national or local schools – mostly working from home as one-person businesses. To cater for this growing market, it has become apparent that there is a need for a book that covers many of the subjects that are not necessarily included in the ADI exams, but which are essential for running a successful driving school and working from home.

This new book – *Practical Business Skills for Driving Instructors* – is primarily aimed at those people who are thinking about starting a new career in driver training and instructors who will be running their own home-based business either independently or as a franchisee. *Practical Business Skills* includes information on starting a new business, working from home, the legal requirements of being self-employed, and an overview of the requirements of the ADI qualification. The book also deals with business opportunities and continuing professional development.

Chapter 1 looks at some of the advantages and disadvantages and pros and cons of becoming a professional driving instructor, with an indication of a few of the main benefits and business possibilities of being self-employed.

The second chapter includes an overview of the DSA exams for new instructors and the ADI check test. The periodic check test is one that all registered instructors must prepare for on a regular basis. It is nowadays much more like a re-examination of your instructional skills and is becoming more and more stringent. This chapter is an overview; much more detailed information about the exams and the check test is in *The Driving Instructor's Handbook.*

In Chapter 3 we deal with the important factors involved in making the decision about working for yourself – whether as a franchisee or as a completely independent sole trader. This chapter also deals with the basics of running a business from home and how to set up the business on a legal and formal basis.

Chapter 4 is all about the financial implications of starting up and running your own business. In particular it deals with organizing the finances of the business and the importance of a properly constructed business plan.

The administration of your new business is covered in Chapter 5; including office administration, bookkeeping, insurance, VAT, National Insurance and tax implications.

Chapter 6 covers the marketing and promotion of your business; how to make sure that the customer care you offer is to a high standard; advertising, sales and promotion; using the professional code of practice and how to deal with the situation when things go wrong.

Driving licences and driving tests for your pupils are dealt with in Chapter 7. This chapter provides important and extensive information about how pupils go about the process of obtaining a provisional licence and the legal requirements involved; details of all aspects of both parts of the L driver test; and an indication of the fees that the pupil will have to pay for their licences and tests.

A lot of new drivers and very often the parents will have questions and queries on many different aspects of the process of learning to drive. Chapter 8 gives an overview of some of the questions you may be asked and an indication of the answer to these queries. Some of the subjects covered in this section are not strictly part of the L driver syllabus, but all of them are essential pieces of information that you may need to provide for your pupils and for potential customers.

Chapter 9 gives a general summary of some of the possible business opportunities available to the professional driver trainer. You may decide to concentrate solely on L driver training and preparing pupils for the driving test, but if you do decide to branch out and widen the scope of your regular work, this section gives an indication of some of the potential areas of work.

Chapter 10 – Continuing Professional Development: CPD should be an essential part of any instructor's work. The DSA emphasize the importance of improving and developing your range of skills – not only with practical in-car teaching and coaching skills, but also in relation to customer care and business skills. This section gives guidance about courses and programmes that are available, particularly from the various trade associations and an indication of further, voluntary qualifications to be considered.

The future

Looking ahead, over the next few years we will see many changes in the area of driver training and testing. As a result of the Driving Standards Agency's recent review of the complete driver training and testing regime several new initiatives have been proposed and are likely to be implemented or phased in over the next few years.

The main proposals in the review include:

- A new 'foundation course', which will be available from schools and colleges. The course leads to a new qualification for young drivers on 'safe road use'. This scheme has now been implemented in several schools and colleges and will be rolled out nationally in the near future.
- A more focused and thorough learning process for the learner driver in preparation for the L test. The emphasis would shift from vehicle control skills to the wider skills needed to be a safe driver, from driving in difficult conditions such as night driving or in poor weather, to learning how to predict and respond to the intentions of other road users.
- A new and revised training syllabus to ensure that learners understand exactly what is required of them at each stage of their development. The syllabus will enable learners to become more responsible drivers by undertaking a structured and efficient learning programme and by being able to accurately assess when they are ready to take the driving test.
- An improved driving test. The new-style test would require the driver to demonstrate independent driving skills and a clear understanding of different situations on the road. An additional feature would be the option of modular assessment.
- New opportunities to take extra post-test training. In conjunction with the insurance industry and employers in industry the DSA will develop new courses and qualifications to be taken after the driving test. This initiative could lead to reduced premiums and a better chance of a career in the 'driving for work' sector.
- A star rating system for professional driving instructors. This system would replace the existing grading of instructors with different criteria including:
    - The instructor's average pass rate on the L test.

- Number of pupils presented.
- Training received by the instructor.
- Services offered by the instructor – for example – 'structured in-car training'.
- CPD. The amount and type of continuing professional development undertaken by the instructor.
- Implementation of the industry code of practice.

It is anticipated that this new system would give learner drivers a better choice of instructor based on pass rates and the level of training the instructor has achieved.

- A review of driving instructor training and testing. The DSA's intentions in this respect are that the instructor should be better able to focus their own initial and ongoing training on those areas of driver behaviour that have the closest link to safe driving and to ensure that instructors are providing a quality service. This is likely to be implemented over an extended period of two to three years.

When these measures are implemented they will make a significant impact on the way instructors organize their training of new drivers and the way in which pupils are prepared for the driving test.

In view of all these developments over the next few years, it is important that all instructors keep up to date with their professional knowledge, expertise and skills by considering all aspects of their 'continuing professional development'.

1

Becoming an Approved Driving Instructor (ADI)

Over 1.5 million people learn to drive each year in the UK. Of these, most are in the age group of 17 to 20. There are currently about 44,000 registered driving instructors, although it is estimated that only 50–60 per cent are involved in driver training as a full-time occupation.

Most instructors these days are self-employed, operating either as small, independent businesses, or as franchisees of one of the larger national driving schools. Some instructors work together in small local groups, but most 'schools' are one-person organizations, usually working from home. The main national driving schools are mainly collections of franchised instructors rather than employed instructors. Within these franchises the individual has the backup of marketing, sales and bookings facilities.

Instructors working for this type of franchise have the advantage of flexibility with their working hours and the opportunity to work from home, combined with a reasonable amount of security through working with a large nationally recognized organization. Various types of franchise are available and there is usually the opportunity to negotiate individual arrangements to suit the individual needs of the franchisee. For example, some franchisors will vary the terms and conditions depending on the level of backup required and the length of service of the franchisee.

Other instructors prefer to work completely on their own account, without the commitment of paying a regular fee; either way, there are now very few 'driving schools' or employed instructors in the conventional sense.

To run your own business – whether it is as a franchisee or as an individual sole trader – you need more than the instructional skills that are tested in the official DSA qualifying exams. Even with a franchise arrangement there is a need to have a variety of skills other than simply the ability to instruct. These skills include customer care, administration and business skills, none of which is in the syllabus for the official instructor qualifications.

As previously indicated, the vast majority of instructors work on their own account, usually with no separate business premises. A few medium-sized driving school businesses exist, but normally most instructors are self-employed or franchised. It is extremely rare for driving schools to employ instructors in the traditional sense, with all the benefits of employment such as National Insurance payments, holiday entitlement, pension provision and so on. This means that most instructors are left to organize their own affairs such as sickness benefit, health care, pensions, holiday pay arrangements and National Insurance contributions. For these reasons, after qualifying as an instructor, you will need to give considerable thought to, and make plans for, running your own business including an assessment of how you will deal with the day-to-day administration of the business.

Remember that you will be responsible for many of the features that would otherwise be the responsibility of the employer. More detail about this aspect of working for yourself is in Chapter 4. Chapter 3 deals with working from home and using your home as an office, while Chapter 5 has information on the administration of running a small business.

WHAT DOES THE JOB OF THE DRIVING INSTRUCTOR INVOLVE?

It is not just a question of riding around in a nice car and giving direction instructions.

Think carefully about what you want before spending £2,000–3,000 on training. To be a professional driving instructor you have to pass three stringent exams. The pass rate for these exams is not very good – 48 per cent for Part 1 (theory), 40 per cent for Part 2 (driving) and 28 per cent for Part 3 (instructional ability).

Your income will depend on a number of factors – do not always believe the adverts that indicate an income of £30,000 per year straight after qualifying. Unlike a job with a regular income, your profit from your business or the franchise you take on will vary from time to time and will be non-existent if you go sick or take a holiday.

TRAINING

Decide whether you need to enrol on a lengthy (and sometimes costly) course for the theory part of the exams. A lot of trainees complete this part of their training by way of home study – either by buying the complete DSA question bank or by using a comprehensive training manual such as *The Driving Instructor's Handbook*. An advantage of doing this is that you can continue with your regular employment while you study part-time. On the other hand some people prefer to take professional training right from the start. This gives some advantages – working in a group of other trainees is helpful in the learning process; working under the tutorship of professional trainers means that help and advice is readily available.

If you decide to study at home be prepared to spend quite a lot of time using the officially recommended books and other materials. Don't, however, make the mistake of reading the study books from cover to cover. Use them as reference materials and structure your learning on a subject-by-subject basis.

CUSTOMERS

Pupils will usually be in the 17–20 age range, although other sources of potential customer might include people who learned to drive in another country and who need a few familiarization lessons, or the person who has not driven for some time and who requires a refresher course.

There are indications that women learners often feel more comfortable with a female instructor. Currently there seem to be slightly more women than men taking the driving test, but only about 20 per cent of registered instructors (ADIs) are female.

COMPETITION

Competition in the driver training industry is quite intense as there is currently no regulation or restriction – either nationally or at local level – on the number of instructors operating in a particular area. Of the 44,000 registered instructors it is estimated that probably only about 50–60 per cent of them are actually full-time instructors, which indicates that there are about 60 pupils for each instructor. To obtain your share of this market, it is worth finding out about existing instructors in your area. This can be done by researching the local business directories, for example Yellow Pages and Thomsons. Other sources of information include websites such as www.learners.co.uk, www.driving-test-success.com or www.driving-schools.co.uk.

Competition for the individual one-person driving school comes partly from other individual instructors in your area, but also from the national organizations such as BSM (www.bsm.co.uk), the AA (www.theaa.com/drivingschool) and the Learner Driver Centre (www.learnerdriving.com).

INSTRUCTOR QUALITIES

To become a professional instructor you will need to acquire the appropriate technical knowledge and skills required to pass the entry exams and to be able to carry out the day-to-day work of driver training. But as well as this specific expertise the role of the instructor requires certain personal qualities. You need to have a calm and approachable manner and the ability to communicate with pupils at all levels. You should be aware of the need for the safety of all road users. This includes yourself, your pupils and other people, particularly vulnerable road users such as the elderly and the very young. You should have the ability to communicate ideas and instructions concisely and clearly, combined with the flexibility to adapt the instruction to the pupil's needs and abilities. You will need to be able to motivate and encourage pupils, using a variety of teaching techniques. Additionally you must be prepared to work unsociable hours, often in the evenings or weekends and must have the ability to concentrate for lengthy periods of time and to observe closely the pupil's actions.

These qualities are expressed by the Driving Standards Agency in their starter pack for potential instructors as:

- good people skills;
- patience and understanding;
- a thorough knowledge of the theory and practice of driving;
- teaching and coaching skills;
- a facility to keep abreast of changes in the statutory regulations that govern the content and conduct of driving tests as well as driving instruction;
- an ability to provide a professional service to people from very diverse backgrounds;
- business sense.

As an experienced and responsible driver, you will already have many of the qualities and attributes to become a professional driver trainer.

Responsibilities

As a professional driver trainer you will have certain responsibilities, including:

- showing proper concern for the safety of your passengers, other road users and yourself;
- an awareness of the need to drive in an economic and environmentally friendly manner;
- being aware of the need for the safety and well-being of your pupils, particularly in the early stages of their training.

Concentration

You will need to have a high level of concentration throughout the working day. As a driver, remember that any distraction from the driving task can be potentially dangerous in today's traffic conditions. More particularly, as an instructor, your concentration is even more important. Read the road well ahead so that you can keep your pupils safe and relaxed and ready to learn.

Anticipation and awareness

As an experienced driver you will already appreciate that predicting what might happen as well as what is actually happening is an important element of driving. As an instructor, you will need to be even more aware of potential hazards in good time so that your pupil can prepare for them. Make sure you plan ahead as far as possible and anticipate potential hazards so that you can allow plenty of time for your instructions and for the pupil to respond appropriately.

You must recognize the needs of each individual pupil and anticipate how each of them might respond to changing situations.

Patience

An efficient and effective instructor shows patience and tolerance towards other road users. Displaying a positive attitude will set a good example to your pupils and help with their driver development. From a professional point of view, demonstrating tolerance and patience, not only with the pupil but also towards other road users will help build your pupils' confidence in you and your ability as a professional driver trainer.

Confidence

As a conscientious and efficient driver you will be displaying confidence at all times. By planning well ahead and anticipating potential hazards, the confident driver avoids the need to make hurried and potentially unsafe decisions.

As an instructor, it is important that you are confident in your own ability both as a driver and in the skills required to help you build your pupils' own confidence.

With your driver training, make sure you avoid any road or traffic situations that the pupil is not ready for so that you help them gradually build up confidence in their own ability.

Knowledge

As a professional driver trainer, you will need to have a sound knowledge of the rules and regulations in *The Highway Code* and *The Official DSA Guide to Driving* and the ability to pass on this knowledge so that your pupils will be able to apply the same principles to their own driving.

Make sure you keep up to date with any changes to the rules, regulations or legislation so that you are able to:

- handle your vehicle sympathetically and in an eco-friendly manner;
- apply modern coaching techniques;
- maintain a safe learning environment;
- offer advice to pupils on driver licensing requirements, basic mechanical principles, and the rules for safe driving on all types of road;
- answer pupils' questions confidently and competently.

Communication

As a driver you communicate your intentions to other road users in a variety of different ways: by the correct use of indicators and arm signals, brake lights, early positioning, reversing lights, horn, flashing headlights, hazard warning flashers and eye contact.

Similarly, as an instructor your instruction skills will involve communicating effectively and in different ways with the wide variety of types of pupil you will be dealing with. Adapt the terminology you use so that all of your pupils understand exactly what you mean.

Communicate with your pupils by:

- establishing the level of understanding of the individual pupil;
- finding the most effective method and style of communication;
- explaining new principles in a clear and straightforward way;
- using visual aids effectively;
- giving practical demonstrations where appropriate;
- developing confidence and success in the pupil by using 'talk through' where necessary;
- giving directional instructions clearly and in good time;
- giving encouragement through positive feedback and praise where deserved;
- asking appropriate questions;

- encouraging the pupil to ask questions.

Awareness

New drivers need to be taught to a high standard, with hazard awareness playing an important part in their development. Teach your pupils to:

- handle the vehicle sympathetically and in an environmentally-friendly way;
- drive with courtesy and consideration;
- look and plan well ahead, anticipating what might happen;
- take early action to avoid problems;
- compensate for other drivers' mistakes;
- understand what they are doing and why they are doing it.

BENEFITS

Before deciding to change your career, consider some of the benefits of becoming a full-time self-employed or franchised instructor.

You can be self-employed and, within reason, you can decide what hours you work. A reasonable income can be generated, but this will depend on your abilities, expertise and experience. By working for yourself there is more opportunity for job satisfaction and knowing that you will have started new drivers on the road to safe driving.

More detail about working for yourself is in Chapter 3.

Full-time instructors can earn about £15,000 in their first year, increasing to around £23,000 to £30,000 a year when fully established.

Your income will be based on the cost of a lesson and the amount of hours you are prepared to work. Lessons are currently being charged at various rates from about £14 to £30 an hour and it is possible to work up to 40 hours or more. Car expenses, running costs, fuel, advertising and other expenses will have to be paid out of the income.

WORKING CONDITIONS

You will need to fit your working hours around your pupils' needs and availability, including evenings and weekends. There will almost certainly be seasonal variations in the available work, particularly around Christmas and the New Year or during the summer holidays.

Lessons normally last between one and two hours, but some instructors offer more concentrated periods of training, including intensive one-week courses.

FRANCHISING

Instructors who work in a franchise arrangement can expect to pay a weekly fee ranging from £200 to £300, including the use of a car. You can expect this amount to be reduced after you have been with the franchisor for some time. Franchised instructors also pay for their own fuel.

The cost of a franchise can vary and will be determined by factors such as: location, hours to be worked and level of support required. As part of the franchise package you could normally expect assistance with new customers and bookings, brand name and promotion, insurance, sickness and holiday cover.

COSTS

Your main initial cost (unless you are signing up for a franchise) will be the provision of a suitable training car. A reasonably small car is preferred by most instructors, as the running costs can be much lower. You will need to allow for the cost of fitting dual controls and an advertising roof sign. Running costs, including road tax, insurance, maintenance and fuel will all need to be allowed for in your budgeting.

As well as insuring the car, you will also need public liability and probably other insurances such as sickness and life cover.

Registration fees and the official DSA exam will cost about £400 to £500, with training fees to be added to this amount.

You will need to budget for marketing, advertising and probably a website as well as the usual business costs including stationery, business cards, headed paper and so on.

YOUR OWN DRIVING

As a potential professional driver trainer you should already be an experienced and proficient driver. However, this may not always be the case; you might have been driving for a number of years without taking any kind of refresher training or assessment. Without realizing it, your driving methods and standards may have changed or deteriorated over the years and you may not have kept up to date with changes in style or accepted modern practices.

This section gives an indication and an overview of some of the points you should be looking for in your own driving before you set out on a programme of training as an instructor. It also offers advice on eco-driving .

In the starter pack for new instructors issued by the Driving Standards Agency (DSA) the emphasis is on how the actual ADI own driving exam is conducted, with only one short item offering advice on how to prepare for the exam or on how to improve your driving to meet the standards required.

To show the DSA that your driving is up to the standard required for inclusion on the Register you need to be able to drive 'to a high standard of competence, demonstrating the principles of eco-friendly driving and a well-planned, positive, progressive drive, adhering to and attaining national speed limits when safe and where possible' – the DSA's own words.

For details of the ADI Part 2 exam ('own driving') see Chapter 2.

Remember that passing the driving test should not be regarded as the end of your learning. Unfortunately, most drivers rely entirely on experience from that point on and rarely take the opportunity to refresh or upgrade their skills and/or knowledge by undergoing any more training, or by formal assessments or appraisal of their driving or by obtaining an additional voluntary driving qualification.

Even if you are an experienced driver, with some kind of additional training over the years, there will almost certainly be room for improvement. For one thing, the DSA's standards and requirements for the ADI exams are generally higher than those of some of the advanced driving organizations.

You may need to adapt and modify some of your techniques to suit the improvements in vehicle design and the changes in today's road and traffic conditions. Remember also that attitudes and generally accepted methods and practices change from time to time. For example, people who have been driving for a number of years often have preconceived ideas on various driving topics – often with outdated misconceptions about modern driving techniques.

A few myths and misconceptions

The most common of these, of course, is the myth that we must always slow down by changing down through the gears. Although this was probably the case many years ago with old-fashioned cable brakes and 'crash' gearboxes, it is totally unnecessary with modern vehicles that have very efficient brakes and five- or six-speed synchromesh gearboxes. With modern braking systems, the emphasis should be on braking effectively to reduce the vehicle speed on the approach to a hazard then selecting an appropriate gear for the lower speed. This will often entail the use of 'block' gear changes from, say, five to three or four to two as appropriate for the conditions. An added advantage, of course, is that both hands will be on the steering wheel while the braking is carried out. This is important as the weight of the vehicle will be more on the front wheels while braking, meaning that the steering will feel slightly heavier.

Remember – 'Brakes are for slowing, gears for going'

Consider what happens when you are approaching a potential hazard. If you need to slow down for the hazard that subsequently clears as you approach you do not necessarily need to change down consecutively through the gears. After slowing, decide on the most appropriate gear for the new speed and then use that gear to keep the car moving and to accelerate away. Keeping both hands on the wheel while you are braking will give more control.

Changing down rather than using the brakes effectively to reduce speed is not good practice and can result in an unnecessary wastage of fuel.

Signals

The Highway Code tells us that signals should be used if they will help to warn or inform other road users of your intentions. It is not generally good practice to routinely give a signal for everything without considering what is going on around us, but many drivers feel that they should give a signal without thinking about who (if anyone) would benefit. The well-known expression 'Mirror-signal-manoeuvre' is often taken too literally without enough consideration on whether the signal is required and, if so, the timing of it. 'MSM' should be interpreted as: 'Use the mirrors as appropriate, decide on whether a signal would be appropriate and, if so, the timing of the signal, followed by the manoeuvre, for example a change of position, direction or speed.' For example, when passing a succession of parked vehicles a right signal might be counterproductive because the following traffic may not then be ready for the signal that subsequently means 'I intend to turn right'. Equally, with the timing of the signal, if we are intending to change lanes and there is a vehicle starting to overtake, signalling too early might confuse the issue and cause the other driver to hold back unnecessarily.

Other examples of where drivers often signal unnecessarily include moving off and stopping. The important issue is to decide whether a signal would benefit someone else, including pedestrians.

However, in most situations, if you are not sure whether a signal would be beneficial, it is generally better and safer to give a few too many signals rather that not enough. Remember that you cannot make a potentially unsafe driving action safe simply by signalling.

Signals given at the wrong time or without considering the effect of the signal can cause other road users to take unnecessary avoiding action, so make sure you observe and think before giving the signal.

Steering

One of the more contentious 'myths' is the one relating to steering. Many instructors, particularly among those who have been around for a number of years, often assume that it is essential for pupils to use the pull/push method of steering. This method of steering was always accepted as the 'norm' with an insistence that the hands must not cross over except when reversing. The reality nowadays is that there is no reason why a 'rotational' method of steering should not be used as long as the vehicle is under complete control all the time. It is interesting to note that most new drivers abandon the pull/push method as soon as they have passed the driving test and are no longer under the 'control' of an instructor. This probably indicates that pull/push is not a natural way of steering. There should, however, be no loss of control by letting the wheel slip or by too much unnecessary one-handed steering. Naturally there will be times when only one hand will actually be steering – while changing gear or reversing in a straight line, for example – and other times when rotational steering will be more efficient and effective.

Try to use your coaching skills with novice pupils to find out how they use the steering with natural movements and then, if necessary, modify the style or method to avoid any serious faults or steering control issues.

Lane selection and discipline

Relying too rigidly on Highway Code advice regarding selection, particularly at multi-lane roundabouts, can lead to potential conflict with other road users in today's congested traffic conditions because a lot of drivers will simply take the lane that seems to give them more of an advantage in making progress. A certain amount of tolerance is needed, combined with effective forward observation and planning together with, occasionally, a certain amount of local knowledge.

Many drivers these days are reluctant to use conventional lane discipline and will use whatever lane seems to them to be most appropriate. This includes turning left from a right hand lane and vice versa. As an experienced driver and a potential instructor you need to be aware and ready to make allowances as necessary to avoid possible conflict.

Defensive driving

Defensive driving involves:

- using an effective and efficient system of car control;
- planning well for all road and traffic situations;
- being aware of the actions of other road users;

- anticipating potential as well as actual hazards and problems;
- being alert to what is happening to the sides and behind you;
- making allowances for other people's mistakes.

It also means driving with responsibility, care, consideration and courtesy.

To quote from the DSA's *Driving – the Essential Skills*: 'Defensive driving is based on effective observation, good anticipation and control. It's about always questioning the actions of other road users and being prepared for the unexpected, so as not to be taken by surprise.'

1. Car control

The basic 'system of car control' involves a routine procedure that is applied in all situations:

- Mirrors – Signal – Manoeuvre (MSM)
- Position – Speed – Look (PSL)
- Look – Assess – Decide – Act (LADA).

On the approach to a potential hazard or if you are likely to change speed or direction you should:

- MSM. Check the mirrors and all around to see what is happening and consider whether your proposed action will be safe. Decide whether anyone will benefit from a signal well before carrying out the manoeuvre.
- PSL. Move into the correct position. Adjust the speed of your vehicle and then select the appropriate gear. Look all around.
- LADA. Look for pedestrians, other vehicles and any obstructions. Assess whether it is safe to proceed. Make a decision to either carry out the manoeuvre safely or hold back and reassess the situation.

2. Forward planning

Many drivers mistakenly think that the quality of their driving is simply a question of their skill in handling the vehicle. Although control of the car is an important element it is the perceptive and hazard recognition skills that have a more significant effect on road safety and the reduction of accidents.

Driving involves a continuous process of attending to, interpreting and responding to the constantly changing traffic conditions. To be able to plan well ahead there is a need to continually check, recheck and assess potential hazards and the possible responses to the hazard.

3. Awareness

The skilful driver is always aware of what is happening all around, including traffic to the sides and to the rear. By continually scanning the road ahead and to the sides, combined with frequent use of the mirrors, you should be aware of other people's intentions and probable movements. Just looking in the mirrors is not enough, however; you need to act appropriately on what you see and how you expect the other person to act or react.

4. Anticipation

Driving safely and defensively involves anticipating and predicting the actions of other road users and recognizing potential hazards.

In most driving situations there are some things that *will* happen and others that *might* happen. Anticipating usually means taking some sort of action when you expect that something will or might happen. Traffic conditions change constantly. Make sure you check and recheck what is happening around you and be alert to any possible changes in conditions.

5. Alertness and observations

As well as planning well ahead, it is just as important to know what is happening to the sides and behind you. Mirrors should be adjusted so that you have the maximum possible view of the road behind you with the minimum of head movement.

Additional 'blind spot' mirrors can be useful, particularly in multi-lane traffic, but remember that mirrors do not always give the complete picture and that you may have to check any blind areas.

6. Making allowances

By showing patience and anticipation you will be able to deal with situations where other people around you might have made a mistake in their driving or are being aggressive or apparently hostile with their actions. In these situations, and with your driving generally, avoid driving in an aggressive or a competitive way. Be ready for, and make allowances for, other people's mistakes by slowing down or giving way – even if you feel that you should have had the right of way.

Eco driving

Eco-friendly driving is now an established part of both the L test and the ADI Part 2 exam.

As a professional driver trainer you are expected to be an experienced driver and will need to show that you have an environmentally friendly approach to all aspects of your driving, including the need for fuel efficiency.

Eco-friendly driving can make a significant impact on the use of conventional fuels, as well as a significant reduction in carbon emissions.

To make an improvement in fuel-efficiency there are several areas of your own driving to consider:

- *Acceleration.* Your use of the accelerator should be steady, smooth and progressive wherever possible, avoiding any unnecessary speed peaks. A smooth driving style can save up to 10 per cent of fuel used.
- *Gears.* Use the highest possible gear for the speed you are travelling at. Lower gears and higher revs will increase your fuel consumption. Cars with manual gears are usually more fuel-efficient than automatics.
- *Braking.* The footbrake should be used in a smooth and positive way, with a certain amount of tapering both on and off. Avoid any harsh use of the brakes by easing off the accelerator earlier when possible.
- *Gear changing.* Make gear changes effectively, with 'block' changes up and down where appropriate. Move into the higher gears reasonably quickly.
- *Hazard awareness and forward planning.* These techniques should be used effectively to minimize any unnecessary or harsh changes of speed or direction.
- *Vehicle sympathy.* Keep engine speeds relatively low whenever possible. Generally, keeping the engine speed to about 3,000 rpm (revolutions per minute) can save a considerable amount of fuel. Use all vehicle controls smoothly to avoid any unnecessary sharp fluctuations in speed.
- *Manoeuvring.* Park so as to drive off forwards. Reversing into a parking space and then driving out forwards is generally regarded as more fuel-efficient than reversing out. You will be making extra demands on the engine if you reverse when it's cold.
- *Speed.* Keep to all legal speed limits and plan well ahead for any changes. It is generally estimated that you can save a considerable amount of fuel simply by reducing your speed by 10 per cent.
- *Air conditioning.* Avoid using air con or climate control unless it is necessary as this can be detrimental to fuel consumption. Avoid driving with the car windows or sunroof open as this can

create 'drag' and an increase in fuel consumption, but let enough fresh air in to keep yourself alert.

Individually these savings may not seem much, but collectively they can make a significant difference, not only to your own costs, but also on the global use of carbon fuels.

More tips for using less fuel

- Plan your journey carefully in advance to avoid travelling more distances than you need to.
- Don't carry more in the car than you need to. Take out of the boot any items that are not needed and that are only adding to the vehicle weight.
- Take the roof rack off when it is not needed. It will only create more drag and make the vehicle less fuel-efficient.
- When you start the engine, make sure you switch off all ancillary items such as heaters, demisters, radio and lights. This helps to start the car as efficiently as possible. Once the engine has started then switch on any items that you really need.
- Check the tyre pressures regularly. If you drive with under-inflated tyres you will use more fuel.
- Have the car serviced regularly. An engine that is not properly tuned will use more fuel than is necessary and will give out higher levels of hydrocarbons and carbon monoxide.

2

The Approved Driving Instructor qualifications

This chapter deals with the registration as a professional driving instructor – the qualifications required and the exams to be taken.

THE ADI REGISTER

To become a professional instructor and to qualify as an ADI, you must:

- Hold a full UK or EU unrestricted car driving licence.
- Have held the licence for at least four out of the previous six years. (A full, foreign licence, an automatic-car driving licence or a provisional licence held after passing the driving test all count towards the four years.)
- Not have been disqualified from driving at any time in the past four years.
- Be a 'fit and proper person' to become an ADI. (All convictions, including motoring offences still in force are taken into account by the DSA.)
- Pass the ADI Register qualifying examinations and then register within 12 months of doing so.

- Meet the current UK restrictions on accompanying a learner driver – that is, a minimum age of 21 and must have held a full car driving licence for at least three years.

One of the regulations of the ADI Register is that you must undergo a check test, which is conducted by the DSA at regular intervals after you have qualified. This test is more formally known as 'a test of an instructor's ability and fitness to give instruction'. Instructors with a higher grading are normally seen at less frequent intervals than those who have a lower grade. More detail about the check test is included later in the chapter.

The Register is administered by the DSA under the provisions of the Road Traffic Act (1991). The Act makes it illegal 'for anyone to charge (either money or monies worth) for instruction in driving a motor car unless their name is on the Register of Approved Driving Instructors or they hold a trainee's "Licence to give instruction" issued by the Registrar.'

THE ADI EXAMS

The first step is to apply to the Driving Standards Agency for a starter pack. The DSA can be contacted at www.transportoffice.gov.uk or by telephone on 0115 936 6666.

All the application forms are included in the pack together with a list of recommended reading materials for the exams.

You will usually need to obtain a criminal record disclosure (CRD) before submitting an application. Details of the CRD requirements are included in the ADI 14 starter pack. You will also need to provide details of two people (not relatives) who have known you for at least two years and who are prepared to give a reference about you to the Registrar.

Acceptance for application to the Register is not automatic. On average, about one in eight applications are turned down because the applicant does not meet the legal standards.

The list of reading materials includes all of the official DSA books (published by The Stationery Office) and *The Driving Instructor's Handbook* and *Practical Teaching Skills for Driving Instructors* (both published by Kogan Page).

Once your initial application has been accepted by the DSA the qualifying exams must be taken and passed in the following order:

- **ADI Part 1** – Multiple-choice theory test, followed by a hazard perception test (you must pass both parts on the same occasion to obtain an overall pass for this part of the ADI exam).
- **ADI Part 2** – Driving ability test. This is an advanced driving test with a high standard of competence required during a one-hour drive. (You are allowed a maximum of three attempts at this part of the exam.)
- **ADI Part 3** – Instructional ability test. This part of the exam is designed to test your ability in teaching and coaching a learner driver. During the test, you must show that you have the ability to improve the student's driving in a wide range of topics and at different levels of driving ability. (As with Part 2, only three attempts are allowed.)

You must complete all parts within two years of passing the theory test.

After passing all three parts, you must apply for registration with the DSA within 12 months.

ADI PART 1– THEORY TEST AND HAZARD PERCEPTION

For the first part of the test you have to answer 100 multiple-choice questions with a minimum pass mark of 85 per cent. However, the questions are grouped into four 'bands' and you have to achieve at least 80 per cent in each band.

Multiple choice bands and subjects:

Band	Subjects covered	No. of questions
1	Road procedures	25
2	Traffic signs and signals	5
	Car control	10
	Pedestrians	5
	Mechanical knowledge	5
3	Driving test	10
	Disabilities	5
	The law	10
4	Publications	10
	Instructional techniques	15

Sample theory test questions

1. *You could use the 'two second' rule:*
   (Mark one answer)

- Before restarting the engine after it has stalled.
- To keep a safe distance from the vehicle in front.
- Before using the mirror-signal-manoeuvre routine.
- When emerging on wet roads.

2. *To help the environment, you can avoid wasting fuel by:*
   (Mark three answers)

- Having your vehicle properly serviced.
- Making sure the tyres are correctly inflated.
- Not over-revving the engine in lower gears.
- Driving at a higher speed where possible.
- Keeping an empty roof rack properly fitted.
- Servicing your vehicle less frequently.

3. *You are following a car driven by an older driver. You should:*
   (Mark one answer)

- Expect the driver to drive badly.
- Flash your lights to overtake.
- Be aware that the driver's reactions may not be as fast as yours.
- Stay very close behind, but be careful.

4. *To avoid an accident when entering a contraflow system, you should:*
   (Mark three answers)

- Reduce your speed in good time.
- Switch lanes at any time to make progress.
- Choose an appropriate lane early.
- Keep the correct separation distance.
- Increase speed to pass through quickly.
- Follow other vehicles closely to avoid long queues.

For more detail on preparing for the ADI Theory Test, please refer to *The Driving Instructor's Handbook*.

Hazard Perception Test

The second part of the test involves 'hazard perception'. This consists of 14 video clips, each lasting about one minute.

Various types of hazard, such as vehicles, pedestrians and road conditions, are depicted. You respond to the hazards by clicking on a computer mouse. The earlier you spot the developing hazard the higher the mark you achieve. Five marks are available on each clip, with a total of 15 scoreable hazards. The pass mark for hazard perception is currently 57 out of 75.

You can take the theory test as many times as necessary.

ADI PART 2 – DRIVING ABILITY

This part of the exam is a test of your own driving ability.

It is far more difficult than the ordinary L test – it is an advanced driving test requiring a high standard of skill and competence. To quote the DSA: 'The test is of an advanced nature and a very high, consistent standard of competence is required. Candidates must show a thorough knowledge of the principles of good driving and road safety and that these principles can be applied in practice.'

The test is in two parts: an eyesight test, followed by a one-hour practical test of your own driving ability. You must pass both parts on the same occasion.

Eyesight

For this part of the test, you will need to be able to read in good daylight a vehicle registration plate from a distance of 26.5 metres (for a new-style plate with eight digits) or 27.5 metres (for an older-style plate with seven digits). Glasses or contact lenses may be worn.

Vehicle safety questions

At the start of the test the examiner will ask several questions on vehicle safety. This part of the syllabus includes:

Steering, brakes, lights, reflectors, direction indicators, audible warning devices, liquids and coolants.

Sample questions:

> '*Show me* how you would check that the direction indicators are working correctly.'
> '*Tell me* where you would find the information for the recommended tyre pressures for this car and how the tyre pressures should be checked.'

'*Show me* how you would change the headlights from dipped to main beam and explain how you would know that the main beam is on whilst inside the car.'

'*Tell me* how you would know if there was a problem with the anti-lock braking system.'

Syllabus

The practical driving syllabus covers:

- moving away straight ahead and at an angle;
- overtaking, meeting and crossing the path of other vehicles and taking an appropriate course;
- turning left- and right-hand corners;
- stopping the vehicle as in an emergency;
- reversing to the right and left;
- reverse parking into a space behind another car;
- reverse parking into a parking bay;
- turning the vehicle to face the opposite direction by use of forward and reverse gears.

In particular, you need to satisfy the examiner on:

- expert handling of the controls;
- use of correct road procedures;
- anticipation of the actions of other road users and taking appropriate action;
- sound judgement of distance, speed and timing;
- driving in an environmentally friendly manner.

The routes used for the test cover a variety of road and traffic conditions, including dual carriageways and motorways where possible.

For this part of the ADI exam you will need to demonstrate efficient car control skills and a high standard of competence with your judgement and forward planning, including hazard awareness.

Controls

Accelerator

The accelerator should be used smoothly and progressively, without any unnecessarily harsh or heavy movements.

Brakes

As with the accelerator, the use of the footbrake should be smooth and progressive.

Ideally, any braking should be done when the car is on a straight course rather than on a bend or corner.

Remember that the footbrake also acts as a signal to following drivers.

Clutch

The clutch acts as a break between the engine and the wheels. If it is used correctly, there will be a smooth transition from one gear to another.

Gears

Use the gears selectively by making 'block' gear changes such as five to three to one, or five to four to two as appropriate.

Bear in mind that, with modern cars, there is very rarely any need for using the gears for slowing.

Steering

Retain complete control at all times.

For normal driving, the accepted method of steering is to use the 'pull/push' technique as this gives control in most situations.

However, with slow-speed manoeuvring and on fast roads with open bends, many people find that this method is not suitable. Whichever method you use, make sure that the vehicle is under complete control at all times.

Judgement and planning

Observation and awareness

Make sure that you use the Mirrors/Signal/Manoeuvre routine and use an effective system of forward observation.

Your scanning technique should ensure that you have a planned approach to any potential hazards rather than having to take action at the last moment.

Hazards

Use your observation skills and the MSM routine to identify potential hazards and to prioritize them.

Some hazards will, of course, require immediate action whereas others might be less important.

Positioning

Your vehicle should be in the correct position on the road at all times.

Your position will enable you to maintain open sight lines on the approach to bends and hazards as well as being an effective signal to other road users of your intended actions.

Lane discipline

Use lane discipline, particularly in roads with several lanes, for example in one-way streets and dual carriageways.

To pass this part of the ADI exam you must:

- demonstrate the principles of eco-friendly driving;
- adhere to and attain, where appropriate and possible, any speed limits;
- demonstrate a planned, progressive and positive drive.

A maximum of three attempts at this part of the ADI exam are allowed.

ADI PART 3 – INSTRUCTIONAL ABILITY

This part of the ADI exam is a test of your ability to give effective instruction. It is generally regarded by most trainees as the most difficult of the three parts of the exam.

The main objective is to assess the quality of your instruction and your ability to pass on your knowledge to a pupil. The test is in two parts – each lasting about 30 minutes. During each part you are asked to give practical driving instruction to an examiner who takes the part of a learner driver. Both parts must be passed on the same occasion.

During the first part your examiner will normally take on the role of a learner driver who is either a novice or is partly trained. For the second part the role to be portrayed would be either a pupil who is at about driving test standard or a qualified driver who needs some form of development training.

For each part of the test the examiner will choose one of 12 different topics as the basis for your instruction:

- safety precautions on entering the car and an explanation of the main controls;
- moving off and making normal stops;
- reversing into limited openings to the left or right;
- turning the vehicle round in the road to face the opposite direction using forward and reverse gears;
- parking close to the kerb, using reverse gears;
- explaining how to make an emergency stop and practical instruction in the use of mirrors;
- approaching and turning corners;
- judgement of speed, making progress and general road positioning;
- dealing with road junctions;
- dealing with crossroads;
- dealing with pedestrian crossings and giving correct signals in a clear and unmistakable manner by indicator and by arm;
- overtaking, meeting and crossing the path of other road users, allowing adequate clearance.

During the test your method and the clarity and accuracy of your instruction is assessed, taking into account the ability of the 'pupil' being portrayed by the examiner. The examiner will also be assessing your observation, analysis and correction of any faults committed by the 'pupil'.

In each part of the test your instructional technique is assessed, including:

- level of instruction;
- planning;
- control of the lesson;
- communication;
- question and answer technique;

- feedback and encouragement;
- your use of the vehicle controls as an instructor.

Remember, you are allowed only three attempts at this part of the exam.

The Part 3 ADI exam is covered in more detail in *The Driving Instructor's Handbook*.

Part 3 exam tips from the Driving Standards Agency:

1. Make sure you have had plenty of training and practice in giving lessons to pupils with varying levels of ability.
2. Listen carefully to the examiner's description of the 'pupil' and to the description of the preset test for each phase of the test.
3. Give positive instruction and guidance to the beginner or part-trained pupil. Use more coaching methods and questions for the trained pupil.
4. Briefings should be appropriate to the 'pupil's' knowledge and geared to the time available. They should relate to the subject matter.
5. You are in charge of the lesson. Watch how the pupil is responding and adjust your instruction accordingly.
6. Respond to the pupil's performance. Correct any general driving faults as well as those relating to the specified exercise.
7. Some driving faults can be dealt with 'on the move'. Apply an appropriate level of instruction for the pupil.
8. Use praise and encouragement where appropriate.
9. Listen carefully to questions and comments when the examiner is in 'pupil' role. Respond appropriately.
10. Do not attempt this part of the ADI exam until you are confident that you can give instruction in all the preset tests to a satisfactory standard.

Both *The Driving Instructor's Handbook* and *Practical Teaching Skills for Driving Instructors* contain more detailed information about instructing and coaching methods.

TRAINEE LICENCE

Once you have passed the first two parts of the ADI exams (the theory test and the own driving test) you may apply for a 'licence to give instruction'. This is not compulsory, but a lot of trainee instructors find that it is helpful as it allows you to obtain considerable instructional experience before taking the third part of the exam. The alternative is to continue with your training and try to get plenty of practice with either learners (but without any payment from them) or with an experienced trainer role-playing the pupil.

To apply for the licence you must be eligible to take the 'instructional ability' part of the exam and not have passed the theory test more than two years previously.

Some stringent conditions are attached to the licence. These include:

- Instruction must only be given for a specified driving school.
- For every trainee instructor at the nominated address there must be at least one qualified ADI.
- At least 40 hours of training with a qualified ADI must be completed within a six-month period before the licence is issued. During the licence period you must either:
  - receive supervision from the sponsoring ADI for at least 20 per cent of all lessons (an accurate record must be kept, and signed, by both you and the supervising ADI);

  or

  - receive a minimum additional 20 hours of training in the topics contained in the training programme. This training must be taken within the first three months of the licence or before your first attempt at Part 3 of the exam. If you fail, you must take a minimum of five hours' additional training.

THE CHECK TEST

After qualifying as an ADI and during your registration you are required to take a regular 'test of continuing ability and fitness to give instruction', which is normally known as 'the check test'. On your first check test after registering as an ADI you will be assessed and graded on your instructional ability on a scale of one to six, with six being the highest and best grade. Higher grade instructors are normally seen at less frequent intervals than those with a lower grade.

During a check test the examiner will sit in on a normal lesson to observe your instruction with a pupil. If it is not possible to provide a genuine pupil the examiner may act as a pupil and will carry out a role play check test where the format is similar to the Part 3 ADI exam.

"The check test is an opportunity for you to have your instructional ability assessed and to obtain professional guidance on any areas where it could be improved." – DSA

During the check test your instructional ability is assessed in the following areas:

Core competencies:

- Fault identification
    - Important weaknesses in the pupil's driving identified. Prioritizing faults.
- Fault analysis
    - Explanation to the pupil of what went wrong and why.
- Remedial action
    - Teaching the pupil how to avoid committing the same fault. Consolidation with practice.

Instructional techniques:

- recap at the start of the lesson;
- aims and objectives of the lesson;
- level of instruction;
- planning of the lesson;
- control of the lesson;
- communication;
- question and answer technique;
- feedback and encouragement;
- instructor's use of controls;
- recap at end.

Instructor characteristics:

- attitude;
- approach to pupil.

ADI grading

As a newly qualified ADI you can expect to be asked to attend for a check test within a few months of passing the qualifying exams. This first check test is regarded by the DSA purely as an 'educational' visit and for this reason it is normal for the instructor to be allocated a temporary 'E' grade. However, if the examiner feels that your instruction is up to a reasonable standard despite your inexperience as an ADI, you may be allocated a grade of four, five or even six.

Once you have been given a grade you can expect to have another check test within a few months if the grade was 'E' or in about two to four years for grades four to six.

On a regular check test if the grading is below four it is regarded as unacceptable or inadequate and in this event the instructor would be revisited in a much shorter time.

Full details of the criteria for instructor grading are in *The Driving Instructor's Handbook* (Kogan Page, 2009).

In my opinion, the general public seem to know very little about the instructor grading system – most people assume that all instructors are qualified and that is about the limit of their interest or awareness. Even if customers are aware of the grades it seems that the general opinion is that 'one' would be the top grade, when in fact, it is the opposite. In view of this if you manage to make the top grade on a check test, make sure your pupils know what it means.

Check test checklist

Looking ahead to after you have qualified as an ADI and when you take your check test (and, indeed, on regular lessons), the following check list will ensure that you have not missed out on essential items:

The car:

- fuel – have you got sufficient fuel for the extended lesson and travel?
- clean and tidy inside and out;
- seat belts (front and rear) working properly;
- tax disc (road fund licence disc) – valid?
- insurance – up to date?
- MoT – if required;
- tyres – are they legal/pressures?
- lights, indicators – are they all working; spare bulbs?
- mirrors – clean/adjustable;
- spare tyre and jack – all OK?
- windscreen washer – topped up;
- L plates secure/visible;
- vehicle documentation.

Yourself:

- clean, tidy, fresh!

Approved Driving Instructor Qualifications

- water, mints;
- spare spectacles?
- sunglasses?

Training aids:

- driving manual;
- Highway Code;
- pens, pencils, notepad;
- visual training aids/diagrams.

The ADI check test is covered in more detail in *Practical Teaching Skills for Driving Instructors*.

INSTRUCTOR TRAINING

Driving instructor training is not compulsory but in practice most trainee instructors feel that they need some specialist help in preparing for the ADI exams.

Legally, any qualified instructor can provide instructor training. There are, however, various voluntary qualifications available as well as different types of courses provided by some of the national organizations. Details of types of available courses and providers are given on page 48.

ORDIT

The Official Register for Driving Instructor Training (ORDIT) is a voluntary registration scheme that was set up by the industry in an effort to regularize the standard of training available for potential instructors. The Register is now administered by the DSA. Entry is dependent on the training organization meeting certain criteria and standards including an assessment by the DSA of the facilities and standards of training offered.

The criteria used for the assessment are based on:

- the level of teaching;
- the trainer's level, type and style of instruction;
- whether the training meets the needs of the individual trainee in all situations;
- whether the training is of a consistent standard.

ORDIT members offer professional facilities and training courses that are designed to develop the skills of trainee instructors and also to enhance the existing skills of qualified instructors. All types of training programmes relating to driver training are included, bearing in mind that quality, and not quantity, is important in any training. Individual trainers can qualify for inclusion on the ORDIT register when they have demonstrated that they can deliver a satisfactory standard of training in one or all parts of the ADI qualifying exams.

When considering training you should bear in mind that simply because an organization is not a member of ORDIT does not necessarily mean that they do not offer a satisfactory standard of training.

The ORDIT Register is one of the ways in which the DSA is taking a positive role in instructor training and is working with the industry to develop and improve the quality of training offered to potential instructors.

For full details of ORDIT membership see the DSA website www.dsa.gov.uk.

PREPARATION FOR THE EXAMS

When deciding on a programme of training you will need to consider what is best for your particular situation and circumstances. Do you need a concentrated course as soon as possible or would a phased programme fit in better with your existing work commitments? You will also need to bear in mind that there is usually a waiting period for the ADI exams and that they have to be taken and passed in sequence. In practice this means that the whole process of qualifying can take several months.

Training to become a professional driver trainer can require a big commitment in terms of the time required to:

- Study in some detail all the recommended books and other materials. Not only will you need to prepare yourself for the ADI theory test, but also to be an effective instructor you will need a thorough understanding of the main principles covered in the syllabus. This means that learning the questions and answers from the question bank will not be sufficient!
- Improve and enhance your own driving skills. You will need to be properly prepared for the ADI Part 2 exam and your driving in the future will need to be at a consistently high standard.
- Invest in sufficient good quality practical training with an experienced and qualified instructor trainer. This is necessary so that you are fully prepared for the ADI Part 3 exam and so that your teaching and coaching skills will help in your role in training better drivers for our roads.

Training courses

The structure of the ADI exams means that you will have to take and pass each part in sequence and there is often a lengthy waiting period for an appointment for the practical exams. You should also remember that should you fail the Part 2 three times you will not be eligible to take the final part of the exam, so there is little point in paying for training that you may not require.

Courses vary a great deal in content, duration and cost. To decide on the one that most suits your needs, get several alternative quotes and find out exactly what you will be getting. Ask for a full description of the syllabus and the format of the training in relation to each part of the exam. The training you receive should be tailored to develop your individual skills in driving and instructing even within a group-training situation.

Various types of training are available and should be considered, according to your needs:

- distance learning programmes for studying at home for the theory test, combined with individual training in preparation for the practical test;
- intensive courses that include preparation for all three parts of the exam in a short period of time;
- courses that will prepare you for obtaining a trainee licence by concentrating on the first two parts of the exam followed by 'work experience' while preparing for the instructional ability test.

Before committing yourself, find out a little more about the structure of the course:

- What proportions of the training will be in-car and in-class?
- How much of the training will be in groups?
- How large will the groups be for in-class work?
- Can the Part 1 (Theory) training be home-based, or will you have to attend at a particular location?
- Will the practical training be on a one-to-one basis?
- Who will be responsible for your training?
- What does the syllabus include?
- Is the training on a fixed timetable, or can it be arranged at times that are more suitable for you?
- If the practical training is shared, how many trainees will be in the car at the same time?
- Does the course allow for the training to be structured to your own particular needs?

- If you opt for working under a Trainee Licence, will you receive proper training, supervision and support as required by the Regulations?
- What qualifications and experience does the tutor/trainer have?

A good training establishment should prepare you properly for each part of the ADI exam. The syllabus should include:

- up to date books and materials with sample questions for the theory test;
- computer-based practice for the hazard perception test;
- sufficient practical training for the own driving exam;
- practical training, preferably on a one-to-one basis for the instructional ability test.

TRAINING AS AN ADI

Before deciding on a particular training course, check out various training providers. Training courses, methods and working practices vary greatly from one training organization to another. Many will ask for a substantial fee 'up front'. If possible, arrange to pay for each section of the training, for example by paying for each part of the exams separately. If this is not possible, at least find out exactly what is refundable if for any reason you are not able to complete the course – for example, what if you are not successful in the practical tests?

Make sure that you do not sign up for training (or pay over any of your hard-earned cash) until you have found out the answers to the questions listed above.

Take a good look at the proposed contract and give yourself time to consider all aspects before making a decision and before signing. If possible, get someone else to check the contents of the contract document.

Course material

To prepare yourself for the exam you will need all the DSA-recommended books:

- *The Official DSA Guide to Driving – the Essential Skills;*
- *The Highway Code;*
- *The Official Guide to Learning to Drive;*
- DL 25 Driving Test report form;
- *The Driving Instructor's Handbook;*
- *Practical Teaching Skills for Driving Instructors.*

Other useful DSA material includes:

- *Helping Learners to Practice – the Official DSA Guide;*
- *The Official DSA Guide to Hazard Perception* – DVD.

Most training establishments will normally provide these necessary materials, but if not they are available from DeskTop Driving and other suppliers. For details of suppliers, see page 220.

Choosing your tutor/trainer or training course

Latest figures show that less than a quarter of applicants who start on the process of training will actually qualify as an ADI. Before committing yourself to spending a considerable amount of money on training, it would be sensible to arrange an assessment with a qualified and experienced tutor/trainer. Obtaining an honest opinion of your suitability as an instructor may well save a lot of time and trouble at a later stage. The assessment should give you a much clearer idea of your preferred method of training.

Training someone to teach driving is very different to teaching learner drivers. It doesn't follow that a good driver will always make a good instructor. Similarly, not all ADIs will have the necessary skills and knowledge to be an instructor tutor/trainer. The ADI may have a good reputation for L driver training, but for instructor training you need someone who has the appropriate qualifications and skills.

The current pass rate for the practical instructional ability part of the ADI exam is under 30 per cent, so it is important that your training is effective and is conducted by someone who is experienced in this specialist field.

When deciding on a programme of ADI training you have a choice:

1. Sign up for a complete programme of training with one of the national training providers.
2. Find out who offers specialist instructor training in your local area.
3. Start off with studying at home for the Part 1 exam by using the official books and other training materials, followed by individual one-to-one training as required for the practical exams.

With each of these alternatives there are advantages and disadvantages.

With the first alternative (1) you need to be sure that you have chosen the right provider; that you will be able to travel to the training centre and that the courses are offered at times to suit you. Try to avoid paying for the complete course in advance and check the details of the course carefully.

The second alternative (2) can be an effective way of training, but make sure you find someone who is qualified and experienced in instructor training – not just a local driving instructor.

The third alternative (3) can be cost-effective and worthwhile, but only if you are able to organize and structure your own study and can find a suitable trainer locally.

When selecting a trainer or training programme there are a few important points to consider and questions to ask:

- Where will the training take place?
- Will it be one-to-one in the car, or will other trainees be with me?
- How much classroom work is involved?
- Who will be my trainer(s)?
- Will I have the same trainer throughout the course?
- What car will be used?
- What if I want to use my own car?
- What car will I be using for the practical tests?
- Is there a reduction in the fees if I use my own car?
- How much will I need to pay in advance?
- What is the refund policy?
- What if I am not able to pass the first two parts of the ADI exam?
- Is there a reduction if I take the Part 1 (Theory) test independently?
- What does the syllabus include?
- Will I have a detailed specification or contract to take away and check before committing myself?
- Will I need to take out a trainee licence?
- What training materials and books are provided?
- Do the course fees include the cost of the exams?
- What about the cost of any retests?
- Is the cost of books and training materials included?
- Are there any training grants or loans available?
- Will I receive extra support if I am not successful in the exams or if more training is required?
- Can I carry on with my regular job while training?

- Will I be provided with sample lesson plans, lesson notes or other handouts?
- I understand that the Part 3 exam is the most difficult. How much of the training will be on 'instruction ability'?
- Will I have the opportunity for mock tests in preparation for each part of the exams?

Instructing and coaching

An overview

During your training to become an ADI you will be dealing with various teaching and learning methods. The most significant trend in this area is to do with 'coaching'.

Coaching is a method that changes the areas of responsibility between the instructor (or coach) and the pupil.

With traditional instructing methods the instructor is perceived as the expert – 'This is what you do', 'This is how you do it' and so on. Coaching, on the other hand, changes this structured format and allows the pupil or trainee to learn in a way that is more suited to his or her individual needs and requirements. By achieving this, pupils are much more involved in the decision-making process and take more responsibility for their own learning.

The use of questions is a major part of the coaching process with the pupil being more involved in discovering the answers, rather than being told to 'do this', 'do that'.

Coaching:
- as a technique is much more relevant to the way pupils learn in today's environment than the rather old-fashioned style of instructing;
- is based on two-way communication with the pupil rather than a more dictatorial approach of telling the pupil what to do and how to do it;

- deals with the possibilities of future success and not so much on past failure or mistakes;
- raises awareness and responsibility in the pupil or trainee, leading to self-awareness and self-confidence;
- is based on the 'GROW' technique and can be applied to driver training with pupils at any stage of their development.

'GROW':

Goal – What do you want to happen eventually?

Reality – What is actually happening now?

Options – What can we do to make changes happen? Are there alternative solutions?

Will – What will you do to make the changes happen?

In driving terms, an example might be:

G – What do you want to happen? – 'Give a smoother ride for my passengers';

R – What is happening at the moment? – 'My gear changes are very jerky';

O – What can we do about it? – 'Improve my accelerator/clutch control; change the timing of the gear changes';

W – What will you do? – 'Do some more practice on accelerator/clutch control and co-ordination'.

This, of course, is only a brief overview of the benefits of coaching – much more detail is given in *The Driving Instructor's Handbook* and *Practical Teaching Skills for Driving Instructors*.

To learn more about coaching methods, you are recommended to read John Whitmore's book *Coaching for Performance* and to look at John Farlam's website www.smartdriving.com.

3

Working for yourself

In this chapter you will find out more about working for yourself; how to structure the business; the benefits of franchising; using your home as an office; your legal obligations; and the business skills needed for working on your own.

There are many positive reasons for starting your own business and becoming self-employed. There are also a few negatives to be considered. You should not consider becoming self-employed if you think that it will be an easy life or that you will make a lot of money without too much effort.

You will be taking responsibility for your own income as well as organizing your income tax, National Insurance contributions and other legal requirements. Self-employment can often be financially and emotionally rewarding, but your business is not likely to take off overnight without a considerable amount of planning followed by some hard work.

Consider some of the advantages and disadvantages before making a move from a secure job:

- you will be free (within reason) to set your own hours of work;
- as a sole trader you have independence from employers – your main area of responsibility is to your customers;
- you will have the opportunity to do work that you enjoy and that you are interested in.

On the other hand:

- you will probably have an irregular and sometimes uncertain income;
- there will be a lack of the usual benefits of being employed – paid holidays, sickness pay, pension contributions;
- there is always the risk of failure.

Before taking the plunge, or deciding whether to 'go it alone' or take on a franchise, it is sensible to get advice from various professionals such as a business adviser, the bank manager or your accountant. They will be able to help you make the move to self-employment. But do not neglect the most important people – your family, spouse or partner. Even the most supportive can be nervous and wary of the irregular hours and uncertain income.

Once you have made the move – be positive, stay focused and maintain your determination to succeed!

In self-employment your own productivity is the most important aspect. You will be able to organize your working day to suit yourself and can have reasonably flexible hours, but only if you are productive when you need to be – generally, if you are not working, you are not earning. If you really are the type of person who is able to take responsibility, make your own decisions and can be disciplined about your new working life, you should be successful.

Starting your own business can be exciting and rewarding but there can be a temptation to rush in and get started too quickly. Most experts advise that you do plenty of research and planning beforehand.

Look realistically at the problems, risks, advantages and disadvantages before making a final decision about going into business on your own account or taking up one of the many franchises that are on offer.

It is not always necessary to have a detailed business plan – unless you are looking to raise substantial capital or if your bank has asked for one. However, it would be sensible to have a simple, one-sheet outline of what you are planning. This straightforward statement should set out not only what you intend to do, but also what you expect to achieve in say three, four, five years' time.

'Going it alone' can be difficult, especially in the early stages. You will almost certainly need the support of close family so before taking the plunge make sure you discuss your plans with them. There can be times of uncertainty, which may well have an effect on your family as well as yourself. Holidays, for example, may have to be postponed or abandoned – especially in the early days.

Your pupils will come from a variety of backgrounds and cultures. Although most learners are probably in the 17–20 age group, you will need to be able to teach customers of all different ages. Remember that your pupils will have varying levels of ability and aptitude – not all of them will necessarily learn quickly or even respond positively to your instruction. Some of them may even have an element of reluctance to wanting to learn to drive – quite a few will feel that the learning process is simply a necessity and their only motivation will be to pass the test as quickly and as cheaply as possible.

As a professional instructor you will need to deal with pupils who may have poor co-ordination and/or a lack of retention of information. Others may have minor learning and physical difficulties. All or any of these situations may well have to be dealt with during your normal working day.

To be an effective instructor you will need to be able to communicate with all types of pupil in a clear, logical and concise manner; be patient when the pupil does not respond immediately or makes repeated errors; and have the stamina and commitment to produce good quality instruction all day, every day.

SELF-EMPLOYMENT

Although being self-employed gives a greater amount of independence than can be achieved by working for someone else, nevertheless there will inevitably be some degree of uncertainty. Make sure that you are not overcommitting yourself financially and, as far as possible, try to finance the business from your own personal resources. Remember that any new business venture carries an element of risk.

Before making any final decisions on self-employment, think about some of the important factors. Look carefully and realistically at the problems, responsibilities and risks involved:

- Carry out a 'SWOT' analysis (see next section for details).
- Establish what competition you will have in your catchment area.
- Make sure you can support yourself and your family during the first few months of your new business. For example, you might decide to retain your regular employment, or find some part-time work, until the business is able to fully support you on a full-time basis.
- Be prepared to take professional advice.

Once you have decided, commit yourself totally to the new business.

STRENGTHS AND WEAKNESSES

SWOT analysis

This is a quick and convenient way of working out your business idea by analysing any strengths and weaknesses (S and W) and comparing these with any opportunities and threats (O and T). Putting these facts or ideas into one document will help you to get a clearer picture.

Strengths:

- What are you good at?
    - instructing/business skills/administration/customer service.

- Is there anything different or better about your service to potential customers?
  - Are you offering something unique?

Weaknesses:

- Do you have sufficient resources?
  - Finances, cash, assets.
- Will you be able to make your business stand out from the competition?

Opportunities:

- Is there room in the local area for a new operator?
- Is there sufficient demand?
- Is the demand increasing?

Threats:

- Are any new competitors likely to come into the market?
- Are you based in an area with a lot of competitors?

Remember that a fairly high proportion of new businesses fail during the early stages, with about one in five of all new businesses folding within the first year of operation. Make sure that your business plan is viable and that you have sufficient resources available.

TIME MANAGEMENT

Most instructors realize that the job cannot be regarded as a 'nine to five' occupation; a lot of customers will be available only in the evenings or at weekends, so you will need to offer lessons at those times. But, to be fair to yourself and to your family, try to set a weekly working timetable that is reasonable and which suits your customers. For example, you may decide to work late on certain days, but with a later start time in the morning on those days. On other days you should be able to allow for a shorter day of instruction, with a break of two or three hours for office work, phone calls, responding to enquiries and so on.

Although you may find that you get occasional (or even frequent!) last-minute cancellations, do not rely on them for your time off or for office work. Cancellations are part of the equation and should be allowed for when you do your initial calculations about income and profit. Similarly, build in regular periods of holiday and allow for them in your costings.

BUSINESS STRUCTURE

There are several main types of legal business structures available to you when starting up a new venture, including sole trader, partnership and limited company. You can always change the structure at a later stage if you want to, as and when the business expands. Most instructors who are thinking of starting a business from home (either as an independent business or within a franchise arrangement) would opt for 'sole trader' status rather than setting up a company. Remember that, even with a franchise, you are still self-employed and therefore a 'sole trader'.

Sole trader

This is the most straightforward form of trading.

Most new businesses start up as sole traders, as it has the advantage of being relatively free of formal and legal requirements. Another advantage is that you do not have to keep too many records, unless you are registered for VAT.

As a sole trader, there is no distinction between the business and your own personal assets. As a result, if the business were to fail, your creditors would be able to make a claim on your personal assets, as well as those of the business. Any assets owned by your spouse would not be affected, but any jointly owned property, such as the family home, might have to be sold so that your share of the proceeds can be used to pay off any business debts.

Even if you employ other people – office staff or other instructors – you can still operate as a sole trader.

If you decide to work for yourself, becoming a sole trader is probably the best option, but remember that you will need to notify the income tax office that you will be changing to self-employment. This applies whether you will be working completely independently or under a franchise arrangement.

Your 'sole trader' business can be operated through your personal bank account, but any personal spending must be identified quite separately from the business payments. It is normally preferred, though, to have separate accounts for personal and business use. Most of the major banks offer special facilities for new, small businesses, so shop around.

If you start up as a sole trader you are self-employed, have no special legal structure and benefit from several advantages of this type of business.

Advantages:
- You can keep simple, unaudited accounts.
- Your National Insurance contributions are relatively low.
- Your Income Tax payments are likely to be lower than if you had formed a limited company.
- Setting up is quick and easy. You simply need to inform the tax and NI authorities.

Disadvantages:
- You are personally liable for all business debts. This means that all your assets could be at risk.
- You are entitled to fewer social security benefits;
- It can be more difficult to sell the business, or to pass it on.

If you go into partnership (see below) with someone else there are similar advantages and disadvantages. Bear in mind that each partner is personally liable for all the business debts – even if the other partner caused them! It is important, therefore, to have a partnership agreement set up professionally and agreed by all prospective partners.

Partnership

If anyone else is involved in your potential business you might want to look into the question of a partnership with them.

A partnership is relatively easy to organize, as it is similar in structure to being a sole trader except that all the expenses and profits are shared between the partners.

To start up you will need to prepare a basic partnership agreement and notify the relevant authorities. The agreement should cover the main areas relating to the business:

- how to share the profits of the business;
- decision-making in both the day-to-day running of the business and general policy;
- responsibilities for sharing the workload;
- how to dissolve the partnership in the event of retirement, ill health or for other reasons.

As with any legal agreement, it would be sensible to take legal advice about the precise contents, as these will vary according to your individual circumstances. For example, the amount of work done by each partner may vary; your individual areas of expertise may be different; and your financial input may not be equal; and your individual drawings from the business may need to be defined.

Remember that if a partner runs into personal financial difficulties or makes a significant error on behalf of the business, his or her share of the partnership assets may be claimed by creditors.

Limited company

Unlike a sole trader or a partnership, the limited company is a separate entity. This means that, in the event of the business failing, any creditors' claims are limited to the assets of the company and not the personal assets of the individual owners.

This type of legal structure is usually more suitable if several people are involved in owning the business, as it is easier to buy or dispose of the individual shares.

There are quite a few tax advantages to having limited company status. As a director of the company you are an employee of the company and will be paid a salary. This entitles you to better benefits than as a self-employed person.

Setting up a limited company can have several disadvantages, including:

- Start-up costs are generally higher. You will need to involve solicitors or accountants and may have to purchase a ready-made 'off the shelf' company.
- Setting up and running a company is more complicated. You are required to register your business with Companies House and to submit detailed annual accounts.

Individual directors of a limited company have certain obligations. They must make sure that the company is operating completely within the law and that all documents are prepared and submitted in a prescribed format. This can be time-consuming and more expensive than operating as a sole trader or in partnership, but is worthwhile if you feel that you need to limit the liability of the business.

A Guidance Note on owning a business is available from Companies House at www.companieshouse.gov.uk and information about the legal structure of businesses is on the Business Link website www.businesslink.gov.uk.

Franchising

Because of the uncertainties of starting up a new, totally independent business and the risks involved, a lot of new instructors decide to take up a franchise. Briefly, this means that you sign up with a franchisor and start work with a readily available supply of pupils. In return for payments weekly, monthly or per lesson you will normally get a car to work with and the backup of national or local publicity and advertising support. As far as your potential customers are aware, you are the local branch of a large concern.

As a franchisee you will normally have less freedom than if you were running your own business, but the advantage is that you will have access to business support, a supply of new customers, marketing and a brand image. In most cases a car will be included in the regular payments.

Taking on a franchise makes the marketing of a business much more effective and on a larger scale than would be possible as a sole trader. This method of starting a new business is much less of a risk.

As well as marketing, the franchisee is normally provided with training and professional services that would not be available to you when setting up completely on your own as an independent trader. The backup services provided by the franchisor would include sales and customer-booking facilities leaving you to concentrate more fully on your main role as an instructor.

This is becoming an increasingly popular way to start on your own, but before deciding on a particular franchise make sure you do your homework thoroughly and carry out detailed research on all the available options.

For example, do not necessarily accept some of the claims about potential earnings that are made by some organizations and be aware that you will not have the same flexibility to change the product or the service that you would have when working completely on your own account.

Before making a decision on whether to take the franchise route, work out if it is the right option for your circumstances and whether it will provide you with the appropriate work/life style that you are looking for or whether you would be better off working as a completely independent instructor.

Franchising – advantages:
- You run your own business within an agreed format.
- You receive ongoing support from the franchisor.
- You benefit from local and national advertising; an agreed format.
- You will normally receive initial and ongoing training and professional development.

Franchising – disadvantages:
- The regular weekly or monthly payments can make a significant difference to your income.
- You must stick to the rules, regulations, terms and conditions of the franchisor. This sometimes limits you in terms of any of your own initiatives.
- If the franchise arrangement does not include 'free' weeks – Christmas, New Year, annual holidays etc, you may find it difficult to take time off.
- You might be restricted in taking on new customers by word-of-mouth and recommendations.
- You could find that you are expected to take on new pupils from too far away, which will give you extra, unprofitable mileage and lost time.
- Your area might be overloaded with other instructors from the same franchisor.

Several of the major national driving schools offer franchise packages that are all quite similar, but with a few variations in the terms, conditions and benefits of the individual package. Some of these franchises offer different types of arrangements within their overall schemes, depending on your individual requirements.

The market leaders in this area are BSM and the AA.

AA driving school

Franchise benefits include:

- a new Ford Focus every six months;
- insurance, road tax, breakdown cover;
- car maintenance and servicing costs;
- replacement vehicle within 24 hours;
- low cost business-rate mobile phone;
- local and national advertising;
- optional pupil introduction charges.

At the start of the franchise arrangement you have a choice of whether you want the AA to provide pupils for you, or whether you prefer to build your business independently by sourcing your own pupils. This means that you can control the actual franchise fee – the more pupils you find for yourself, the lower the franchise fee you pay each week.

For longer serving instructors, loyalty rewards include free sickness and accident cover, substantial discounts on the franchise fee, franchise-free periods and free branded clothing.

Contact details:

Web: www.theaa.com/driving-school/driving-instructor.

Tel: 0800 587 0086.

British School of Motoring (BSM)

BSM offer a similar type of franchise arrangement, with flexible payments depending on whether you supply your own pupils.

Main benefits:

- alternative fee options – fixed, variable and associate;
- manual or automatic Fiat;
- car replaced every 16,000 miles;
- national and local support, with 90 town centre offices;
- free 'continuing professional development';
- reduced franchise fee for longer serving instructors;
- fee-free week at Christmas;
- extra fee-free weeks after 12 months;
- flexible working arrangements.

BSM offer three different types of franchise package.

Fixed fee:

For instructors who want a complete package, including a supply of pupils. Suitable for someone wanting to work full time and to maximize their earnings. Discounted fees and extra fee-free weeks for longer service.

Variable fee:

For those instructors who want more flexibility in the number of hours worked, but with the convenience of having pupils supplied. The franchise fee is directly linked to the number of hours worked.

Associate franchise:

For instructors who want the advantage of a BSM package, but who will source their own supply of pupils. This package offers the benefit of a reduced, fixed weekly fee.

Contact details:

Address: BSM, 2610, The Quadrant, Aztec West Business Park, Bristol, BS32 4TR.
Web: www.bsm.co.uk/instructor-centre.
Tel: 0845 851 9688.

Other national franchises are available, for example from LDC and RED, as well as numerous local organizations offering a variety of different types of franchise arrangements.

Contact details:

LDC
Web: www.learnerdriver.co.uk.
Tel: 08000 740 886.

RED Driving School
Web: www.training.go-red.co.uk.
Tel: 0800 688 8811.

Franchising checklist

Franchising arrangements vary hugely, particularly with a more locally based organization rather than one of the national companies listed above. Some have a fixed weekly fee, which may include a car, supply of new customers and a lesson-booking facility as well as local advertising and promotion. Others operate a system of paying commission on each lesson, while some schemes involve a combination of the two.

Before committing yourself to a particular franchise, check out a few important details to find out exactly what you will receive and what you are expected to pay for.

- The car:

    Does the fee include all expenses other than fuel? Will the vehicle be replaced at regular intervals? Is a back-up car readily available in the event of breakdowns or an accident? If you are expected to use your own car (for instance on a commission system) will the net income be sufficient to pay for a replacement at the appropriate time?

- The contract:

    What is the minimum term? What arrangements are in place for exiting from the contract? Are there any guarantees about the amount of work available? Are you allowed to find your own customers? If you decide to leave, will the pupils be allowed to move with you?

- The work:

    Are you guaranteed a minimum number of pupils? What geographical area would you be expected to cover? Do you have any control over this? Would there be a reduced weekly fee if the level of work dropped? Are there any 'fee-free' weeks (Christmas, New Year, annual holidays, etc)? How many other franchised instructors will be working in your area?

Franchising – a summary

Taking on a franchise gives you the opportunity to effectively set up your own business, but without the problems associated with starting up on your own from scratch. You will be using a well-known brand and can benefit from the expertise and support of the franchisor – that is the company who offer the franchise.

As a franchisee you can enjoy many of the benefits of being self-employed with much less risk attached to it. With a good franchise operation you will normally get full support in terms of a supply of new customers, promotional material and pupil record systems.

Before deciding whether to take up a franchise you probably need to ask yourself a few questions:

- Why do I need a franchise? Can I go straight into running my own business?
- What is my turnover likely to be?
- Will I be able to cover my franchise fee and still make a decent living?
- What if things go wrong and I don't get the level of business I expect – will I still be liable for any franchise fees?
- What is different about this particular franchise?

LEGAL OBLIGATIONS

There are special legal guidelines and definitions about working for yourself and whether you are strictly 'employed' or 'self-employed'. For example, to be legally self-employed you must be free to choose what work you do or what hours you work and you must be able to allow someone else to do the work on your behalf. If these criteria are not met, or if all your work is with one company, the tax authorities may at some point decide that you are not genuinely self-employed and would then expect payment of income tax, National Insurance and so on as if you had been employed.

ADVANTAGES AND DISADVANTAGES OF SELF-EMPLOYMENT

An employed person would normally have a whole range of benefits available to them as part of their employment. These benefits would include holidays with pay, sickness and maternity benefits, National Insurance contributions and PAYE income tax calculations and deductions. Quite often an employment package would include extra holiday entitlement for longer service, private health care provision and contributions to a private pension scheme.

On the other hand, the self-employed person has the responsibility of organizing and funding all of these for themselves. Loss of earnings during time off for holidays and for sickness must be allowed for; National Insurance contributions have to be paid by the individual rather than sharing the cost with an employer; and allowance must be made for times when the work is not available – bank holidays, weather conditions, vehicle breakdown and so on.

WORKING AS A SELF-EMPLOYED INSTRUCTOR

After qualifying as an ADI, the only continuing check on your ability is the periodic check test conducted by the DSA. This looks only at your ability to deliver a specific lesson to a specific pupil on the specified date. In other words, it's only a 'snapshot' of your overall instructional ability. At the present time the DSA are not involved in checking on your skills relating to customer care or to your ability to run a business legally or efficiently. In fact, when members of the public occasionally query the business conduct of a particular instructor or organization the DSA response is that they are only concerned with the level of instruction given. This leads to a situation where most instructors think that the ADI check test is the only thing they must concern themselves with.

This situation should change over the next few years as a result of several projects that are currently under way. In particular, one programme is looking at all areas of instructor refresher training, and most of the main trade organizations such as the Motor Schools Association are actively preparing themselves to offer the appropriate courses as soon as the requirements are known.

To be an effective all-round instructor – especially if you are working on your own account or with some franchises – you need to develop any of your skills that will enhance your business and keep you fully up to date in all areas, not just instructional skills. Equally important in the current era of consumer rights, customer care skills are becoming ever more important. Business skills – including legal issues, cash flow, insurance responsibilities and public liabilities – are necessary in running a business today.

As a qualified ADI you are likely to be working either as a completely independent instructor or as a franchisee. Either way, you are in effect running your own business as a self-employed trader. In these circumstances there is a need for you to be fully conversant with many of the requirements of running a small business. Just how much you need to know will, of course, depend on the working relationship between yourself and your franchisor where applicable. In running a small business – particularly in a service industry where there is direct one-to-one contact with your customers – you should also be aware of the need for customer care qualities, standards and responsibilities.

BUSINESS SKILLS

Management and planning

Running a business from home can offer several financial advantages. If you use one of the rooms as an office you are able to claim for the expenses such as rent, heat and light. This is in addition to the normal running costs such as telephone, computer, stationery, office staff and so on. However, remember that there will be a certain amount of administrative work: you will need to keep appropriate records to satisfy not only your franchisor, but also the tax and National Insurance authorities.

Take into account that you will not necessarily be able to work all year – you will need to make allowances for time off for illness and for holidays.

Make sure that you understand and make provision for life and health insurance, your pension, savings and any sudden or unexpected downturn in business.

Check whether you would require planning permission to operate from your home address. Find out whether there are any restrictive covenants or lease restrictions that might apply.

Administration

You will need to keep proper records of all your business transactions, especially for income tax purposes and where VAT is involved.

Whether you need to employ an accountant, either to set up a system for you or to deal with your end-of-year affairs, will depend on the type and size of business you run.

If you employ someone part time to deal with these matters (your spouse or partner, for example), you can claim those expenses against tax, but you will also need to make the necessary payments for tax and National Insurance.

Bookkeeping and accounts

To keep accurate records of your business (particularly for tax purposes) you would normally be required to keep details of all income and expenditure including purchase invoices and cash payments. There are plenty of relatively simple systems available either in manual or in computer form. As a minimum, most businesses will need bookkeeping records for purchases, sales and cash payments.

From your records you need to know:

- how many lessons were completed in any particular period;
- what your running costs are for each lesson;
- what profit you have made;
- what monies are owed to your business customers;
- how much the business owes;
- what your cash flow is likely to be;
- what the business's bank balance is at any time.

Any bookkeeping records, including invoices and payments, that you use should be retained for five years after 31 January following the year of assessment.

Tax affairs

Taxation can depend on whether you operate as a sole trader, in a partnership or as a limited company.

Self-assessment for income tax purposes requires the taxpayer to retain his or her business records to support the information given on the tax return. The tax return should be submitted before 30 September if you complete the form manually, or by 30 January if you fill in the forms online.

For details of self-assessment for the self-employed, visit www.hmrc.gov.uk or telephone 0845 900 0444 for advice.

Pension planning

Recent surveys have shown that millions of people do not make sufficient provision for their pension requirements and that a significant number make no provision at all. This is a situation that is likely to be even more important in the future, as there are signs that the state pension system will have to change drastically to cope with future demands. One of the changes might involve an increase in the pension age.

Right from the start you should make adequate provision for your pension by charging the right rate for your services to allow for an appropriate regular payment into a pension scheme. Take appropriate independent advice from a registered broker or adviser, as there are many suitable schemes available. Remember that a large proportion of the payments you make can be offset against tax.

For information and details about state pensions or for a prediction of your pension at retirement age, contact the Pension Service on

0845 3013 011 or at www.thepensionservice.gov.uk, quoting your National Insurance reference number.

VAT

If your annual turnover is more than £70,000 (for 2010/11) you will need to register for VAT. Even though you will then need to charge VAT for all your services, there are some benefits, as you are allowed to claim back the VAT on many of your expenses.

For details about VAT, go to www.hmrc.gov.uk or contact the advice line on 0845 010 9000.

Finance

When you start up a new business it is usually necessary to have sufficient funds available to cover the cost of purchasing vehicles and other equipment. There will also be a need to have access to sufficient funds to support yourself (and your family, if applicable) for a period of time until you generate a regular income. Of course, if you decide to take out a franchise some, but not all, of these expenses will be covered by way of weekly or monthly payments, rather than as capital expenditure.

Financing assets

Manufacturers and retailers usually offer finance packages and will often encourage you to make use of them. Many of these schemes are worthwhile – particularly if there is a genuine special low-cost offer available. However, it is important to shop around for loan arrangements from other sources. It may, for example, be more cost-effective to borrow the money from your bank, a building society or a specialist finance firm. In this way you may be able to tailor the repayments to suit your particular circumstances.

A popular way of financing is to use contract hire, where you do not necessarily own the vehicle, but you do know exactly what your repayment costs will be over a fixed period.

Another fairly common method of paying is by a 'finance lease'. This involves making a payment at the end of the term based on the anticipated value of the car. This method reduces the initial payment and the monthly repayment costs and also provides the opportunity to purchase the car for a predetermined cost at the end of the leasing period.

Hire purchase and lease purchase are other viable alternatives, with some similarities. With both methods you do not legally own the vehicle until you have finished paying all the required instalments.

National Insurance

As a self-employed person you need to pay National Insurance at the flat weekly rate and also a Class 4 contribution based on the level of your profits. If you employ any staff, you will need to pay the employer contribution for them.

Banking

You don't necessarily need a business bank account as well as your normal personal account, but it is usually quite useful as a means of completely separating all your business income and expenditure. If you decide to use a personal account, make sure that you keep details of all business transactions quite separately.

When opening a new business account, shop around to find the most appropriate bank. Many banks and building societies offer reduced charges or even free banking for the first one or two years of a new business.

4

Starting up a new business

In this chapter you will find information about setting up the new business; why you need a business plan; financing; cash flow, profit/loss and budgeting; the driving school car.

When starting your own business or in the early stages of taking on a franchise, work may be relatively slow in building up. You need to allow for this and for the fact that there may well be several weeks of low or moderate income. Don't always believe all the stories and adverts indicating that an income of £25–30,000 is available from day one – most of this type of publicity is aimed at generating new trainees and potential instructors for the training organization.

Even when your business or franchise is well established you will need to plan for periods when your income may be reduced – holidays, sickness, for example – and for times when business is traditionally weak – around Christmas and in the summer school holiday period.

Right from the start you need to know what you want from the business and how you want it to develop. A business plan will be important in this respect, not just when you are looking for funding.

BUSINESS PLAN

There are two quite separate reasons for producing a business plan:

- one is for presentation to the outside world – particularly if you are trying to raise funds from an external backer such as a bank or other financial organization;
- the other is for your own internal use so that you can monitor the performance of the business over a period of time and make adjustments accordingly.

Some small business advisors suggest that you should have two quite separate plans – the first one will be much more conservative in its estimations than in the internal one. With both plans, however, the figures should be realistic and justifiable.

Business plan checklist

- unless you have a strong plan you will probably find it difficult to obtain start-up funds;
- a properly constructed plan will serve as a structured means of linking your business to any investors such as the bank, mortgage provider or private investor;
- the preparation of a business plan focuses your thoughts and gives a clearer indication of success;
- the plan can provide ongoing information about the progress of the business and will be a measure of the business's performance;
- having a business plan in place will enable you to prioritize what you need to achieve and the timescale to work to;
- compiling a business plan will enable you to organize and plan your cash flow.

A business plan will help you to set out your goals and plan how you can achieve them:

- be clear about your objectives;
- keep the plan brief and concise;

- check it through thoroughly;
- prioritize what you need to do;
- keep it flexible;
- define your product and service accurately.

In Chapter 3 we mentioned a SWOT analysis of your own qualities in deciding whether to start in business. This type of analysis is equally important for the business plan.

Strengths and weaknesses are usually relating to you and your business – your skills, the quality of the service you offer.

Opportunities and threats are usually related to external influences such as whether a type of market emerges or new competition appears on the scene. Completing a SWOT analysis is a way of clearly identifying key issues in the business plan.

Strengths:

- How and why are you likely to be successful?
- What do you do well?
- In what way do you see your particular business standing out from your competitors?
- Have you any definite advantages?

Weaknesses:

- Is there anything that will limit your business's performance?
- What aspects of running the business do you not do well?
- Indicate how you will deal with these issues.

Opportunities:

- What customer needs are not currently being met by your competitors?
- Are there any particular new markets to exploit?
- Are there any potential new areas of growth?

Threats:

- Are there any trends in the industry that could reduce the amount of business available?
- Are your competitors likely to respond to your activity in the market?
- Will any new competitors come on the scene?

After completing your SWOT analysis, try to be realistic in appraising your strategy. Can you use your strengths and minimize any weaknesses? How will you overcome your weaknesses so as to minimize the effect of any potential threats?

Within your initial business plan include all possible variables for each item and try to work on the basis of realistic figures rather than 'what if'. These figures should include:

- car – purchase price, depreciation, repairs, maintenance, tyres, cleaning, fuel, dual controls, advertising signs, insurance, tax;
- ADI registration fees;
- bookkeeping and accountancy (including insurance for extra accountancy in the event of HMRC investigation);
- office equipment – telephone (including mobile), computers and printers (including repairs, maintenance and replacements), stationery, postage, internet and broadband;
- health insurance;
- personal pension;
- advertising;
- income tax and National Insurance;
- bank charges.

Constructing the plan

Start with a summary. Although this is the first page, leave it until you have completed the rest of the plan. This gives the reader the opportunity to see what the plan is all about without necessarily reading through the complete document. Use the summary to highlight the key points of the plan.

Background information. If you are starting out as a self-employed sole trader you need to explain who you are, your qualifications and experience. Explain how this fits into the requirements of the business.

Give the location of the business and how this fits into the potential customer base.

What your service is all about. Outline what you will be offering and how it will fit into the proposed market. Who will your customers be, and how will you pitch your fees? Suggestions about pricing your lessons are given in the next section.

Marketing plans. This section should describe how you will identify your market and how you intend to reach that particular market. Indicate what the competition is likely to be.

How you will operate on a day-to-day basis. If you will be operating from home, identify how you will keep a balance between the business and your social life. For example, if you are likely to be out on the road most of the time, who will be dealing with enquiries and admin? Your marketing budget should be indicated, with an explanation of how you will promote the business to potential customers.

Financial assessment, projection and likely needs. This part of the plan should define how much start-up finance you are likely to need, what the cash flow might be for the first year or two, the profit and loss forecast for two or three years; and what assumptions you have made on any of these. Attach the detailed documents here.

Risk assessment. Complete a detailed SWOT analysis.

Pricing your lessons

Decide on your pricing:

- What do your local competitors charge?
- Do you want to be the cheapest around?
- Or more exclusive and be regarded as better quality?
- What will you charge?

CHECKLIST FOR START-UP

- Identify your strengths and weaknesses.
- Decide what steps you need to take.
- Research your customer market.
- Check out the competition.
- Decide what will be different about your service.
- Find out about professional advice and support.
- Set realistic targets.
- Understand what books and records you need to keep.
- Know about your tax and legal obligations.

To ensure that your business has sufficient working capital, especially to cover unexpected costs, make sure that you are able to keep up to date with the business's current financial situation. Although the bank statements can give a reasonable guide, they do not necessarily represent the true picture, partly because they are usually issued monthly. Internet banking can be better in this respect, because it gives a more up to date figure, but uncleared cheques and regular payments may not have been added.

To keep the business's financial position fully up to date always keep a record of all payments received and payments made.

BUDGETS AND CASH FLOW

To set an effective budget, you will need to produce a relatively simple cash flow forecast. This can be done either manually or by using a computer program. The forecast should be for a full 12-month period but with a breakdown of the figures into monthly amounts. Each month should show the budgeted figure with a separate column for actual receipts. There are plenty of software programs available, but a simple paper-based system might be more appropriate for a small home-based business.

Cash flow forecast – example:

		January budgeted	actual	February budgeted	actual	March budgeted	actual	etc
Opening bank balance (see note 1)								
Income								
	Lessons (see note 2)							
	Other income (see note 3)							
Total receipts (A)								
Expenses (see note 4)								
	Car –							
	fuel							
	insurance							
	repairs							
	maintenance							
	leasing							
	etc							
	Office –							
	heat/light							
	rent							
	rates							
	water							

	January budgeted	actual	February budgeted	actual	March budgeted	actual	etc
phone							
stationery							
postage							
computer/ internet							
bank charges/ interest							
bookkeeping/ accountancy							
etc.							
Franchise fee (if appropriate)							
Personal drawings, wages (see note 5)							
Tax/ national ins. (see note 6)							
Capital expenditure (see note 7)							
Advertising							
Travel /meetings							
Fees – ADI							
associations							

	January budgeted	actual	February budgeted	actual	March budgeted	actual	etc
professional							
Etc.							
Total expenses (B)							
Balance (A-B)							
Closing balance (transfer to start of following month) (see note 8)							

Cash flow forecast – notes:

(cross ref to numbers in chart on pages 82–84)

1. Opening bank balance. This is the amount of money actually in the business account at the start of the month. When you are starting out, this amount will normally be nil unless you have specifically put money into the account or you have an arranged overdraft. If you have an overdraft the amount should be shown in brackets.
2. Cash from lessons. Most of your lesson sales will be cash payments, but include any advance payments from pupils (for a series of lessons, for example).
3. Other receipts. Put in here any sales from books, CDs, etc.
4. Cash purchases. Estimate the amount you will have to pay to suppliers – fuel, repairs, insurance, franchise fees, etc.
5. Wages/drawings. In this section you will put any personal drawings or payments to other people for wages.
6. Tax and National Insurance. Your own payments for NIC and income tax go here. If you are a sole trader your Class 2 NIC payments will be made monthly and your income tax twice yearly.
7. Capital expenditure. If you are likely to buy any equipment such as a replacement car or a more up to date computer system, put the amount in here. If you are buying on HP or with a loan, enter the amount of the deposit and the individual monthly payments separately.
8. Closing balance. Add the 'total receipts' amount to the opening balance and take away the 'total payments' to work out what the closing balance will be.

If there are any noticeable differences between budgeted and actual figures take appropriate and prompt action. By doing this, you should be able to make sure that the business does not spend more than can be covered by the current balance.

PROFIT AND LOSS PROJECTIONS

Keeping a profit and loss forecast up to date will enable you to work out how much the business will earn over an extended period of time. Profit is not the same as cash flow – even if the business is making a profit, it is still necessary to make sure that you have cash available when you need it in the short term.

The forecast can be done on a simple spreadsheet, either manually or with a computer, showing all budgeted and actual sales and expenses on a month-to-month basis.

Profit/loss projection – example:

	January Budgeted	Actual	February Budgeted	Actual	March Budgeted	Actual	Etc
Sales (a)							
Less:							
Car expenses							
Personal drawings							
Gross profit (b)							
Office costs							
Travel							
Fees							
Depreciation							
Bank charges							
Etc							
Total overheads (c)							
Trading profit (b – c)							
Interest charges (loans/overdraft etc)							
Net profit (before tax)							

As well as conventional bank loans and overdrafts, there are various loan schemes available including the Enterprise Finance Guarantee (EFG). This is a joint venture between the government and various commercial lenders. Loans are usually available to new and start-up businesses.

Further details are available from the Department for Business, Innovation and Skills (www.bis.gov.uk) and Business Link (www.businesslink.gov.uk).

Business Link is a government-sponsored business advisory and support service. It is available online and through local advisers.

Your local Business Link can be located by phoning 0845 600 9 006, or by entering your postcode on the website www.businesslink.gov.uk.

This is a really useful starting point for anyone wanting to set up a new business. As well as providing information and advice, the service puts you in contact with experts in your local area.

Business Link can help you:

- manage your business;
- find and retain customers;
- comply with current legislation;
- find events and local support.

Once you are committed to setting up your business, the Business Link interactive start-up organizer can help with the nuts and bolts of getting the business off the ground. It does this by taking you step by step through a series of questions about your business, followed by a personalized list of tasks to undertake. The final stage of the start-up organizer gives you access to a library of resources to assist you.

LOANS, GRANTS AND FINANCE

To find out if you are eligible for a government grant or a loan, you will need to be prepared to provide detailed information about the nature, history and financial position of both yourself and your business. This information would normally include:

- an up to date business plan (including potential funding arrangements);
- financial forecasts (profit/loss and cash flow);
- an indication of the business's current position.

The decision-making process is carried out by individual lenders on a commercial basis. The government has no influence over this decision making, but does offer guarantees to the lending body.

Other sources of funding, by grants and loans, include local and regional support through Local Enterprise Agencies (LEAs), Regional Development Agencies (RDAs) and the Department for Business, Innovation and Skills (BIS).

Contact details for these organizations are in the 'Business contacts' section in Appendix 1 (page 217).

For details of government initiatives, see www.bis.gov.uk.

Grants

There is a wide variety of grants available to new businesses, but the application process can be quite complicated. For details, start by checking the 'Grants and support directory' section on the Business Link website (http://www.businesslink.gov.uk/bdotg/action/gsd).

Any application for business funding will require you to provide a comprehensive business plan describing your proposed business in some detail. For details of constructing the plan, see page 78.

If you apply for start-up funds (a grant or a loan), you may well feel that it would be worthwhile using a professional business adviser who will guide you through the application process and who will make sure you include all the necessary and relevant detail.

To give yourself the best possible chance of getting the funding you need, there are a few important points to follow:

- Check the eligibility guidelines carefully. Make sure you are applying for the most appropriate funding and that your project qualifies.
- Give all the required information as accurately as possible – even if you think that it is unnecessary.
- Use realistic figures – not guesses.
- Put as much information as you can into your business plan, but give a brief overview at the start.

Loans, overdrafts

A lot of banks offer free banking for small new businesses and most will offer competitive rates for start-up loans. Do not just approach your own bank, but make sure you shop around for the most suitable deal. It is not always a good idea to have all your personal and business arrangements in one place or with one bank.

If you are applying for a loan, make sure that your figures are accurate and realistic. Better to be conservative with estimates of sales and realistic about expenses, rather than being over-optimistic.

Remember that this will be a loan and that it will have to be repaid at some time!

Having a business overdraft can be sensible practice, as long as you are able to pay back the funds in a reasonable amount of time. Whether you use two separate banks for business and personal accounts, or if you use one bank for both, try to arrange separate facilities for each account so that you can retain control of both sets of finances.

Overdrafts can be relatively easy to arrange, especially when you have a healthy financial situation, but remember that the bank can withdraw the arrangement at any time – possibly when you can least afford to repay it.

Credit cards

Having credit cards for business and personal use can be an effective way of paying, but only use them for very short-term borrowing. Try to make sure that you pay off the balance each month and treat any spending as if you were using cash or your current account. Avoid letting the total amount drift, because credit card borrowing can be hugely expensive and if you are not able to pay off a reasonable amount on a regular basis you can be left with some very costly payments longer term.

Professional and Career Development Loan (PCDL)

You can use a CDL to help you gain training and qualifications. The loans are available through an arrangement between several commercial banks and the Young People's Learning Agency (YPLA). The LSC pays the interest on the loan to the bank while you are learning and for one month afterwards. You then repay the loan over an agreed period at a fixed rate of interest. These are loans to obtain a particular qualification, rather than loans to set up a business, but can be useful for a range of courses related to running your business.

More detail from www.direct.gov.uk/en/educationandlearning or phone 0800 585 505.

Finance

If you do not have sufficient resources of your own to start your business you will have to consider how to raise the cash. Sources of extra financing might include your own family or your bank.

If you borrow cash from family or friends there will be a few advantages and disadvantages:

- the lenders are not likely to require guarantees or security for the loan;
- any profits you make will stay in the family or with friends;
- if you are not able to pay back the money promptly or on time the relationship might suffer;
- personal friends or family members might want to get involved with the day-to-day running of the business.

Other means of financing are usually available and you may be able to spread the costs by leasing or renting your vehicles and other equipment. If you are seeking this extra funding, work out how you will repay the money out of your future income and how long it will take. Any kind of borrowing, particularly from a bank, is likely to be more expensive than you realize and you may well be expected to put some of your own money in.

To present your case effectively to a potential lender draw up a complete schedule of:

- why you need the money;
- how much of your own money you intend to put in;
- exactly how you intend to repay the loan, including the interest;
- what period of time you will need the money.

Banks are not the only lenders of money to small businesses. Take advice from your building society, your accountant or a financial adviser about other sources.

Whoever you approach will require a detailed breakdown of your expected income and expenditure, so you will probably need to produce a brief business plan. The plan should include:

- a clear statement of the service you will be offering;
- projection of sales, based on realistic research;
- what your initial requirement will be, as well as any possible ongoing needs;

- how much cash you will be providing;
- basic information about your start-up costs and regular outgoings;
- a profit and loss projection showing how the business will make a profit.

THE DRIVING SCHOOL CAR

Unless you are working under a franchise, the instruction car or cars will be the most costly item of expenditure in setting up your new business.

The choice of school car is often a very personal decision for someone starting their own business and can be a contributing factor in deciding on a particular franchise. However, in order to make an informed choice remember that the decision should be based more on what is best for the business rather than on what car you would like to drive.

Remember that the school car is your daily workplace, so you need to be completely comfortable with the type of vehicle you choose. This should be balanced against the needs of your pupils, the manoeuvrability, economy and to a lesser extent on whether you will need the car to double up as family transport.

There will be times when you will need to carry extra passengers so don't be tempted to choose something that is too small. For all these reasons, most instructors have a small to medium sized vehicle such as a Ford Fiesta, Vauxhall Corsa, Peugeot 207, Fiat 500 or something similar.

The car (or cars) that you use will project a lot of information about you and your business and the image you want to portray. I remember some years ago a particular instructor had a car that was quite distinctive, with eye-catching, colourful, but professional looking, body signs. As a result, many people thought that it was part of a fleet of vehicles, when the reality was that it was the instructor's only vehicle. This approach would not suit everyone, and you may feel that something more discreet would be more appropriate for your style.

There are two ways in which the car can be financed – you can either buy or rent. Each method has its own advantages and there are various ways of financing each of them.

Buying

Cash purchase. If you pay outright for the car you can either finance it from your own savings or by obtaining a bank loan or overdraft. If you use your own savings make sure that you are not using funds that might be needed by the business at a later date.

An overdraft, although it might offer lower interest rates, can be risky as the bank can demand repayment at any time. A bank loan, however, can be for a fixed period of time and at an agreed rate. You will also get a tax allowance on the interest paid on the loan.

Hire purchase. This can be a more expensive way of purchasing than by bank loan because the interest rates tend to be higher. From time to time vehicle manufacturers and dealers offer special rates to driving schools for hire purchase, but remember that you would not actually own the vehicle until all payments have been made.

Lease purchase. This type of contract allows you to purchase the vehicle at the end of the lease period. One of the advantages is that the initial payment will be relatively low, but the monthly payments will normally be higher than with hire purchase. Interest costs will probably be higher because the money is outstanding throughout the complete lease period.

As with any type of payment made over a period of time, the interest element is allowable against tax.

Renting and leasing

As an alternative to purchasing – cash, hire purchase or lease purchase – you may want to consider renting your vehicle(s). This can be done in several ways.

Leasing. This method of renting can be advantageous in that it frees up any capital for other purposes and that tax relief is available on the payments. With a conventional lease you never actually own the vehicle, but with some arrangements you will have an optional residual value to pay. In this case you are able to either purchase the vehicle at that stage or hand it back to the leasing company.

Contract hire. In the early stages of starting a new business this method of financing a driving school car can be an attractive option because of the low initial cost. However, under normal circumstances it can be more expensive in the longer term. Contracts can be simply for the supply of the vehicle, or may include dual controls, road tax, insurance, maintenance and tyres.

The VAT element is often not included in a quoted price, because the hirer assumes that the business is VAT-registered, so remember that this is an extra cost if you are not registered.

Choice of car

Selecting the right tool for the job is important. The initial cost for purchasing or financing the vehicle will be a major consideration, but the residual value and depreciation costs will be just as important. This is probably one of the reasons that a lot of new instructors opt for the franchise arrangement, where all vehicle costs except fuel are covered by the weekly fee.

After fuel costs, depreciation is likely to be the next highest expense for the self-employed independent instructor. Remember that you will have to find the difference between the residual value of the car you sell and the cost of the replacement vehicle.

Depreciation is, therefore, an important part of your decision about the purchase of an appropriate car and is also a major factor in assessing the running costs and should be taken into account in all your calculations on budgets and cash flow.

Just because a particular vehicle is offered by a manufacturer or dealer at a substantial discount does not necessarily mean that it represents the best value. If the residual value after, say, two or three years is very low it could be poor value compared with a slightly more expensive model that has less depreciation.

When looking at your overall business expenses over a period of time, remember that it is the replacement costs that are important, rather than simply the value of the vehicle you are selling. For example, if you were to buy a car for, say, £10,000 and it depreciated by 50 per cent over two years, you would need to find £5,000 plus the extra cost of the replacement vehicle – probably a total of £7,000 to allow for an increase in the sale price of the new vehicle.

The perfect driving school car probably does not exist and your choice of car will depend partly on whether you need the school car to be used for family and social needs apart from the business use.

When you are trying to decide on a particular car, take plenty of time in test-driving different makes and models before making a final decision. The drive should cover the sort of areas that you would be using for training and tests. Check the vehicle for visibility at junctions and on reversing manoeuvres. Be very careful about the interior layout and try to look at the vehicle from the point of view of the pupil. For example, the seating position, the ease of adjustment and the range of positions.

To arrive at a decision on the type of vehicle, take into account some of the other main costs:

- *Insurance.* Check the insurance grouping and potential cost of insurance as both of these items can vary quite considerably.

- *Fuel.* Consider the anticipated fuel consumption of the vehicle. This will have a significant effect on your overall costs owing to the higher mileages involved with driving instruction.
- *Maintenance.* Find out about the cost and frequency of servicing. From time to time some manufacturers and dealers offer servicing as an inclusive part of the purchase price.
- *Warranty.* Decide whether an extended warranty would be beneficial. Some manufacturers offer longer warranty periods than others and with most vehicles you can purchase an extension of the original warranty.

New or used?

There can be a considerable price difference between the costs of new and used cars. Depreciation is usually higher in the first year of the car's life than with an older car. By buying a one- or two-year-old car and replacing it after a further two or three years you will lose much less on the deal compared with buying new and replacing the vehicle after, say, two years. Often the 'nearly new' car will have the benefit of the residue of a warranty still in place.

Against this, many people feel that they would like a completely new vehicle, especially for business purposes. This again is where the franchise has a lot to offer, because you get a new car every few months.

Manual or automatic?

Offering lessons on both manual and automatic cars can be a good selling point for your school, but there are disadvantages. You will have to be careful about juggling your diary to avoid having to change cars too often, for example in the middle of the working day. On the other hand, having two cars available means that one can be used for your instruction work and the other will be free for your spouse, partner and family members.

Remember that pupils who pass the driving test in a car with automatic transmission will have restricted licences.

Dealer, auction or private?

If you buy from a main franchised dealer you get the security of a good warranty, a full service history and the backup of the dealership, but you would normally pay a little more for these benefits.

Large, national auction sites such as ADT or Central Motor Auctions offer good used cars at a substantial saving. Usually these are ex-company cars and can be bought at not much more than 'trade' price. There is a certain amount of consumer protection, but you need to be able to make a prompt assessment of the car before committing yourself in the auction.

With a private sale, you can sometimes pick up a bargain, but remember that you have less consumer protection.

Other places to buy nearly new cars can include internet sites and 'motor marts'.

When setting your budget for the new car, bear in mind that depreciation and replacement costs will be the most important parts of the financial equation.

Equipment and extras

As well as the cost of the actual car, take into account that you will need to purchase a range of 'extras' and pieces of equipment including:

Roof signs and decals. These should be professional-looking and eye-catching as they are an important part of your advertising and presentation to potential customers. Make sure that both the name of your school and the phone number are prominent and that there is not too much clutter or unnecessary detail. Several companies provide signs at reasonable cost. See page 220 for suppliers.

Dual controls. Several types of dual control are available, but the most common ones are rod operated. The cost of supplying and fitting dual controls can be a significant amount, so check out the various alternatives. A list of suppliers is on page 220.

Extra mirrors. These are necessary for all-round vision and for checking on the pupil's use of mirrors, but do not clutter the windscreen with too many unnecessary obstructions.

Cushions. For shorter pupils who might need a raised seating position for better all-round visibility.

High visibility jackets. Two sets of hi-vis vests or jackets in case of breakdown or accident.

Wet-weather clothing and umbrella. For both you and the customer.

Breakdown cover. Although cars are much more reliable nowadays, there will be times when you may well need insurance cover for possible accidents and breakdowns. The cover should include a replacement vehicle so that you are not out of work for an unnecessary length of time. Make sure you have the contact details and membership number readily available.

First aid kit/fire extinguisher. It is a personal choice whether you have these pieces of equipment on board, but at least consider a small first aid kit to include plasters, scissors, paracetamol and so on.

Cleaning materials. For use on the inside and outside of the car. A small hand brush or vacuum cleaner; ice scraper and squeegee.

Spare bulbs. Make sure you know how to change lights and indicator bulbs so that they can be replaced at short notice – at the test centre, for example.

Tyre pressure gauge and tread depth tool. Not only for checking on the condition of the car, but also for instruction purposes.

Local area maps and/or SatNav. For locating new customers and in case of traffic diversions.

Mobile phone. But make sure you do not use it while driving or instructing.

Warning triangle. For advance warning in the event of a breakdown.

When you have decided on the type of car (and whether to fund it yourself or take on a franchise), make sure you keep it in a good, clean condition at all times as the car can be your main advert to current and potential customers.

5

Business administration

This chapter gives information about running your business – the legal requirements, tax matters and the implications of running the business from your home address. You will also find detail on insurances, VAT, health and safety, bookkeeping and accountancy.

Starting your business by working from home can be the easiest and least expensive option, but remember that you will need to check with various people and organizations before you start. For example, you should find out from your landlord, mortgage provider, insurance company or local authority if there are any restrictions about using your home as an office.

If you only use your home as an office base for your business there would probably be no problem, but if you have a steady stream of customers, vehicles parked or anything else that might inconvenience or upset your neighbours, there could be objections. Remember that if you set aside a particular room as an office you will be able to claim business expenses on it, but if the use is extensive you might have to pay business rates on part of the building. There could even be capital gains tax implications if and when you sell the property.

If you are likely to have customers visiting you – for theory lessons or for bookings and so on – you will need public liability insurance to cover for any accident they might be involved in. You will also need to take appropriate steps to ensure their health and safety.

USING YOUR HOME AS AN OFFICE

Planning permission

To run a business from home you would probably not need planning permission unless you will be making substantial changes to the building and as long as you do not inconvenience your neighbours particularly with excess noise or traffic movement.

Mortgage or landlord's permission

Check the conditions of your mortgage and whether you need to obtain permission from your mortgage provider or landlord if you do not own the property outright. Even if you own the property you may need to make sure that there are no restrictive covenants in the title deeds.

Insurance

Although your normal house and contents policy will probably cover the basics, it is unlikely that this will provide sufficient cover for your business needs, so let your insurer or broker know what you are planning.

Neighbours

As well as complying with the rules and regulations about using your home as a base for your business, it makes sense to keep your immediate neighbours in the picture about what you plan to do, especially if there is going to be an increase in traffic or visitors.

Expenses and allowances

If you set aside a particular area of your home as an office, you will be able to claim a reasonable amount against tax, but be careful that this does not have the effect of changing your Council Tax liability to business rates or that you will have a Capital Gains Tax implication on selling the property.

If you are considering using a largish part of your house, say as offices, reception area, classroom and so on, you should take professional advice from an accountant and also from HMRC on how to calculate any potential liabilities.

OFFICE ADMINISTRATION

Wherever you decide to base your business you will need an 'office', even if this is only a spare room or the kitchen table. You need to have a system so that you are able to deal effectively and efficiently with enquiries by phone or e-mail, write and answer letters, deal with customer records and do your bookkeeping.

Your home-based office should ideally be a separate, dedicated room or area rather than a corner of the living room or the kitchen table to avoid potential conflict between business and family affairs.

You will require a supply of stationery, including headed paper, plain paper, envelopes, 'comp slips' and business cards.

Remember that all stationery and printing costs can be charged to the business so long as they are wholly related to business use.

A PC or laptop, combined with a decent printer, is an essential piece of equipment for your office, particularly for printing your own brochures, leaflets, handouts and other promotional material. Even if you are not completely computer-literate you will almost certainly find that a family member or friend will be able to assist in this area. The 'must-have' items of software for the computer will include a good word processing package – for correspondence, pupil records, assessment reports and so on – and a basic accounts package will be worthwhile for your bookkeeping and finances. Use anti-virus software and anti-spyware programs to minimize any security issues. It is important to back up all your important data regularly – either to another PC, a memory stick, external hard drive or to discs.

Computer systems

The use of information technology has become an important part of everyday life in most businesses. In setting up and running your business, make sure you understand, and can specify, exactly what you want from the computer.

IT systems are getting more advanced all the time and it is easy to be attracted by the latest technology.

Your computer system needs to be capable of coping with:

- Word processing: sending out personalized letters, mailshots, handouts, progress sheets and reports.
- Accounts: specialized software packages for small businesses can simplify the process of producing regular and annual accounts.
- Databasing: recording information about your customers and enquiries, but make sure that you comply with requirements of the Data Protection Act (1998). If you have any doubts about this, see www.informationcommissioner.gov.uk or phone 08456 306 060 for more detail.
- Communication: the ability to send and receive e-mails and access the internet via a broadband connection are both important elements of the IT system.

Begin by making a list of what tasks you need the computer system to do. Do not make the mistake of buying an expensive machine that you don't really need. Set yourself a budget and don't go above that figure. Concentrate on what you really need your computer system to do – there's really no point in buying a top-of-the-range system for most normal small business needs.

Buying the computer

You can source your computer system in a variety of ways.

Mail order firms offer a wide range of products at competitive prices, but advice is limited. Returning any faulty goods can be complicated and time-consuming. Make sure you choose a supplier registered with the Mail Order Protection Scheme. This means that you will be covered if the firm goes bust.

Shops and *stores* usually have various systems for you to try out before you buy. Retailers normally offer maintenance and support, but it can be expensive – and the quality of the service can vary.

Manufacturers sell systems over the phone or via the internet. This can be an effective way of buying if you know exactly what you want and do not need advice.

Consultants can specify, install and configure the complete IT system for you. This may be a sensible option, especially if you lack the technical expertise. It is also a good way of establishing contact with an expert to look after your system and to offer ongoing support.

Computer checklist

- Work out exactly what you need and buy a system to suit, rather than being persuaded by sales staff.
- Make sure you have some readily available technical support and build a good working relationship with your computer expert. This support should be from a suitably qualified person who can be available at short notice.
- Use regular 'housekeeping' programs on the computer to make sure that the system is functioning efficiently.
- Protect the computer against viruses and hackers; use passwords to restrict access.
- Create a backup system by using a separate hard drive or discs. Have a procedure for making regular or complete backups and back-up any really important data each day.
- If possible, keep a separate computer for your business – especially if there are children in the house!

- Be wary about downloading programs from sites that you do not know.
- Keep stocks of important items – paper, ink cartridges, memory sticks and discs.

Mobile technology and IT

When you're out and about on lessons you will often have times when you cannot get back to the home office for catching up with the necessary admin, for contacting customers and dealing with enquiries. Nowadays there are plenty of options available.

Netbooks: These small computers (with screen sizes from 5" to 12" or so) are lightweight, portable and are designed mainly for e-mailing and accessing the internet. Expect to pay about £200 to £300 for a machine with a decent specification.

SmartPhones: There are several good smartphones available, including Blackberry, iPhone, Nokia, Palm and other manufacturers. As well as making phone calls, you can access the internet, receive and send e-mails as well as downloading many useful applications.

Wireless: Most broadband providers offer wireless connection as part of the overall package, but if not you can buy an efficient router for a reasonable price. With wi-fi it is possible to connect to the internet from any PC, laptop or netbook as well as linking up wirelessly with other peripherals such as printers and scanners. Wi-fi connection means that you can work from different locations.

Internet phone: This software, from Skype or VoIP, allows you to make calls over the internet. Calls are a lot cheaper than conventional phones, and can in some cases be free.

Software: Finally, have a look at free software. You will be surprised at the wide range of programs that are now available. Take a look at www.opensourcewindows.org for examples of word processing, databases, spreadsheets and other useful business programs.

Telephones

Obviously a telephone will be important to your business. Ideally, try to separate your personal and business calls by having two telephone numbers. If possible, have someone available to answer the phone all the time. If this is not an option, either have calls diverted to your mobile or an answer machine facility will be necessary. Try to get one that can be accessed remotely. The problem with each of these alternatives is that you will probably not have direct contact with a prospective customer, which could mean a lot of missed opportunities, so try to ensure that you have someone answering the phone – at least during normal working hours.

A mobile phone will probably be essential for communication as you will be spending a considerable amount of time out of the 'office'. The phone might be useful so that other people can get hold of you and for emergencies, but remember that it is illegal to use a hand-held phone while driving.

E-mail is, of course, a 'must' for most businesses. Create a separate e-mail address for private use and make sure you include details on all your business stationery.

HEALTH AND SAFETY MATTERS

The Health and Safety at Work Act (1974) is mainly aimed at preventing accidents and providing a safe working environment for employees. However, the regulations apply equally to the self-employed, who have a responsibility for their own safety.

Any business, however small, has a responsibility to provide a safe and healthy working environment for themselves, their employees and anyone visiting the premises. This should not be too much of an issue, but remember that you have an obligation to your customers and yourself in terms of safety and creating a safe working environment.

If you have any concerns, or need further information, you could check with the Health and Safety Executive on their help line, 08701 545500, or e-mail them at hseinformationservices@natbrit.com to find out which regulations might apply to your particular situation.

Full details of the requirements can be found at www.hse.gov.uk.

The Health and Safety at Work regulations apply to all businesses, even if you are self-employed and working from home. Most of the regulations are straightforward and usually based on common-sense procedures.

One point to remember is that if you have a sound health and safety policy in place – particularly if you 'employ' someone to help with office work or as an extra instructor – you may be able to achieve better terms with your various insurances.

You are normally expected to comply with the Regulations by carrying out a risk assessment that would include:

- identifying any potential hazards that might harm you (this includes car and 'office');
- deciding if anyone else might be harmed (clients in the car, visitors to your office);
- assessing the risks and taking appropriate action to reduce them;
- keeping records of your assessment.

As part of the Health and Safety Regulations, remember that it is illegal to smoke in a business vehicle, such as the driving school car, that is used by more than one person. This applies even if only one person is in the vehicle.

More detail can be obtained from HSE:

Tel: 0845 345 0055.
Fax: 0845 408 9566.
Address: HSE Infoline, Caerphilly Business Park, Caerphilly, CF83 3GG.
Web: www.hse.gov.uk.

VALUE ADDED TAX (VAT)

VAT is chargeable on all goods and services if the annual turnover of the business is more than £70,000 (2009/10). If you are working from home and running a small business you will almost certainly not exceed this figure unless you are employing other instructors.

If your annual turnover is likely to be less than £70,000 you are not required to register for VAT, but you can do so voluntarily if you prefer. There are a few advantages to be gained by registering, because you can then claim back the VAT on all your purchases, including cars, fuel, repairs, office equipment, computers and so on. The downside of registering is that you would have to charge VAT on all your lesson fees. The current rate of VAT (March 2010) is 17.5 per cent.

Registering for VAT has another disadvantage in that you need to complete quarterly returns by itemizing all income, expenditure and the VAT element of all transactions. For these reasons, most people prefer not to register unless their annual turnover exceeds the threshold.

More detail about VAT can be obtained from HMRC at www.hmrc.gov.uk or from the advice line on 0845 010 9000.

INSURANCES

Insurance is a necessary expenditure giving cover against a variety of mishaps. For example, you can, for a price, insure yourself or your business for almost any risk including professional indemnity. The main one to consider, of course, is the vehicle you use for training. If this were out of action for any length of time because of an accident it could be disastrous to your income. Shop around to obtain the best deal, but do not necessarily go for the cheapest option – make sure that you get the cover you need.

Business insurance

To make sure your business will keep running even if you are not there to work in it, take out an adequate amount of personal insurance. If you are ill, have an accident or go on holiday your business will stop earning, so check with different providers for insurance tailored to your needs. You may find that one of the trade associations or your local chamber of commerce can offer specially subsidized schemes. Similarly, some of the national organizations such as the Federation of Small Businesses include insurance for the self-employed as well as other membership benefits.

Motor insurance

Although third party insurance is usually regarded as the minimum requirement, for your business of driving instruction it is essential to take out a fully comprehensive policy. Remember, though, that 'fully comprehensive' does not always mean what it implies. Terms and conditions will vary from one policy to another and with different insurers.

Some of the main points about motor insurance to consider include:

- Don't always look for the cheapest cover. The last thing you want is to be without your training car for any unnecessary periods.
- Do you need breakdown cover included? Consider whether it would be more cost-effective to buy this cover separately.
- Legal expenses. If you are involved in an accident where there is dispute about liability, would you benefit from legal expenses cover?
- Excess. Most policies give you the option of paying the first £100, £200 or more of any claim. This can have the effect of reducing the payments, but check whether this amount varies depending on who is driving. For example, some insurance companies might impose a higher excess for young learner drivers.

- Other drivers. If other members of your family will be driving the car regularly, make sure that they are included as 'named drivers' to avoid any doubt in the event of a claim.

Personal insurances

Other insurance should cover you as a provider of income, by taking out life, critical illness and accident cover. You might also feel that you need cover against loss of income – for example, if your car were to be out of action for a long period of time owing to a breakdown you would need to recover the loss of income. Most of these types of cover can be arranged under a composite business policy that is tailored to your needs. This would normally cover other elements such as public and professional liability.

You should consider whether private health insurance would be appropriate to your needs. If you required hospital treatment or a prolonged period away from work, would it be more efficient to your business if you could decide when it would be more convenient to take the time off? This can often be a worthwhile alternative to the NHS waiting periods, although you will need to balance the advantages against the potential cost of private medical insurance, which can vary greatly from one provider to another, and depending on individual circumstances.

If your home-based office is important to the business, check that your house insurance covers the business use and the contents.

To run an efficient business, whether you are operating under a franchise or completely self-employed, you need to make sure you are adequately insured against all potential risks.

For example, your car is the most important item for your business – and you would need to have a replacement readily available in the event of an accident or breakdown. This is not always covered adequately with some insurances or franchise arrangements.

You need to assess your individual situation and decide which of these would be appropriate for your new business.

Life insurance. It is important to provide cover for your dependants to pay any business loans or debts and for them to have sufficient future income.

Your mortgage may provide an element of life cover, but if your business is dependent on you it would be sensible to top up the cover to provide an adequate level of income.

Health insurance. You should at least take out some form of personal sickness insurance to cover the situation when you are unable to work because of an accident or illness.

Private health insurance can be expensive and you will need to decide whether it is appropriate for your particular circumstances. One of the advantages is that you can decide when to take time off for treatment or an operation, rather than being completely dependent on the NHS. You may feel that this is important to your business needs.

Office contents. Although most home contents insurances include limited cover for office equipment used for your business, do not necessarily assume that the amount will be sufficient if you are running your business from a home office. Some policies, for example, will exclude items such as laptop computers; other insurers offer specific policies for working from home. This type of policy would typically include office equipment, loss of cash and cover for any loss of income.

If you do decide to rely on your normal house contents policy make sure that the insurance company is aware that you work from home and specify any particular items of value.

Employer's liability. This type of insurance covers you against any claims from employees for injury or health problems arising from their employment with you.

Although employer's liability insurance is not strictly necessary unless you actually employ other people – other instructors or office staff, for example – it might be appropriate to include your spouse, partner or any other family members who do any work for you.

Public liability. As a driving instructor most claims against you would normally be covered by your motor insurance, but there may be times when you are involved in non-motoring claims. For example, if you have customers using your home or office. Public liability covers this type of claim in the event of an accident.

Professional indemnity. Consider whether you need this type of insurance to cover any claims against your professional negligence.

When you start your business (and particularly as it grows) you will need to check that you have the appropriate amount of cover for all types of insurance. It is sensible to use an insurance broker or adviser at an early stage to make sure you are adequately covered.

Insurance checklist

- Shop around for the best quotes.
- Seek advice from your trade association or chamber of commerce.
- Identify all the risks that the business might face.
- Make sure your business is adequately insured.
- If you employ anyone, get employers' liability insurance.
- Keep a level of perspective – you need to insure yourself against things that might harm your business.

INCOME TAX

As a self-employed person you are, effectively, an unpaid tax collector on behalf of the government. You will need to keep detailed records of all your income and expenditure and to account for them on a yearly basis through the self-assessment system.

When you switch from being an employee to self-employment – as an independent or as a franchisee – the way in which you pay tax will also change. You will need to inform HM Revenue and Customs (HMRC) within three months of starting the business about your new status and you will then be required to pay your income tax on the 'self-assessment' system. The appropriate forms (CWF1) can be downloaded from www.hmrc.gov.uk or by calling the helpline for the newly self-employed on 08459 15 45 15.

The self-employed

When you start the business you will normally have a period of about 18 months or so before you actually have to make a payment. This is not a 'tax free' period, though – you will get a tax bill for this period eventually. This will consist of the tax due for the first year of trading plus an additional 50 per cent 'on account' for the following year. You then continue to make payments at six-monthly intervals.

Self-assessment

Sole traders and partnerships are required to complete a self-assessment form each year.

You will need to submit your self-assessment income tax returns to HMRC each year and pay tax based on your current year's profits. Remember that you will need to put money aside during the year so that you can pay the annual tax bill twice yearly, in January and July. For example, if you make a *profit* of £30,000 you pay tax on that amount, even if you only draw, say, £15,000 during the year. Profit is the turnover of the business less the allowable expenses.

If you had previously been an employee you will have had your income tax deducted at source. As a self-employed person you have to get used to the idea of putting money aside for tax purposes.

The income tax year runs from 6 April to the following 5 April and depending on the start date of your new business you settle your bill by making three payments initially. You would make two interim estimated payments ('on account') on 31 January and 31 July in any particular tax year, followed by a final payment (or, perhaps a refund!) in the following January.

With the present tax system it is your responsibility to work out the amount of tax to pay, but HMRC will do the calculations for you provided you complete the tax return early enough.

If your business turnover is less than £30,000 you now only need to complete a simple three line statement on the self-assessment form showing income, expenditure and profit. You do, however, need to keep detailed and accurate records in case of an audit or a detailed investigation by the tax office.

Key tax dates

(example)

31 January 2010
First instalment of tax for 2009/10 due;

31 July 2010
Second instalment of tax 2009/10 due;

31 October 2010
Deadline for sending 2009/10 tax return in paper form;

31 January 2011
Deadline for filing online version of tax return for 2009/10;
Final balancing payment for 2009/10, together with first instalment of tax for 2010/11.

31 January 2016
You have to keep your business documents for seven years, so by 31 January 2016 you can dispose of your 2009/10 documents.

When you first start the business there will not be any interim payments for a year or so because you will not have a previous history of profits to show. So if you start the business in, say, June you will receive a tax return in the following April, with the first payments due in January of the next year. At that time you would pay all the tax due for your first year of trading plus the first interim payment (half of the first year's payment) for the following year's trading.

The amount of tax you owe is calculated after deducting legitimate business expenses and personal allowances from the total income of the business. As a self-employed sole trader you can deduct many of your business expenses such as overheads, travel, subscriptions and so on.

Expenses and allowances

You can claim items as a business expense for tax purposes only if they are 'wholly and exclusively' for the business. These expenses include:

- Any items you buy to use:
  - In the car. Any equipment you need; for example, cleaning materials, safety equipment and replacements.
  - In the office. Stationery, postage, printing, computer equipment and supplies.
- Any goods you buy to sell on to the customer – books, CDs, DVDs.
- Running costs of the office. Repairs, maintenance, phones, internet connection, computer software.
- Advertising.
- Home expenses. A proportion of your home expenses such as council tax, heat, light, repairs.
- Subscriptions such as DSA fees and professional or trade associations.
- Travel. Legitimate travel costs and living expenses for attending meetings, seminars, workshops.
- Car. Running costs of the car – tax, insurance, repairs, maintenance and breakdown cover.

- Staff. Costs of employing staff, including family members, provided you can show that the work is actually done and at a normal rate of pay.
- Bank charges on your business account.
- Bookkeeping and accountancy fees.
- Interest on loans or business overdrafts (including arrangement costs).
- Business insurance.

For details about employing other instructors, see the section at the end of this chapter (page 122).

TAX ALLOWANCES

The main expenses that are allowable against tax include:

Office

A reasonable amount for use of your home as an office can be set against tax. This can be a proportion of heating, lighting, rent and council tax costs.

Running costs. Telephone, advertising, stationery costs, postage, computer equipment, repairs and replacements can be claimed so long as the expense is necessary and is wholly related to the business.

Vehicle costs

Fuel, repairs, maintenance and additional equipment such as roof signs and decals are all allowable expenses.

Wages and salaries

If your spouse, partner or another family member does secretarial, bookkeeping or similar office work for you the salary can be claimed against your income tax liability. If this is the case, you should draw up a simple, straightforward statement or agreement to avoid any unnecessary queries from HMRC at a later date. The agreement should cover the type of work involved, the number of hours worked and the appropriate salary and holiday entitlements.

Business insurances and subscriptions

As well as the payments for your business insurances (and, of course, your ADI fees), you can also claim for annual subscriptions to any national and local trade associations.

Business loans and overdrafts

Interest (but not the actual expense) on loans and overdrafts can be claimed.

Training and travel expenses

Expenses that are wholly related to the running of the business – meetings, seminars, workshops, for example, can be claimed.

For all expenses make sure that you retain all appropriate receipts.

NATIONAL INSURANCE

As a self-employed person you will almost certainly be responsible for paying National Insurance contributions. These are normally based on a fixed weekly or monthly payment, together with an annual amount depending on your business profits. If you employ other people – instructors or office staff – you will have to pay a proportion of their NI contribution. Even though the payments are more, you will find that the benefits for the self-employed are often less than those for someone on PAYE. For example, there will be a reduced retirement pension.

Your liability for National Insurance will be dealt with when you first notify HMRC about your new status as self-employed. The money will normally be collected by direct debit on a regular monthly basis.

As well as regular Class 2 payments, you will also pay Class 4 contributions if your annual profits are above a certain level. These contributions are collected twice yearly along with your Income Tax liability and are calculated on a sliding scale depending on the actual profit.

National Insurance Contributions

The two types of National Insurance Contributions (NICs) outlined above are currently (2009/10):

1. If you earn more than £5,715 each year you pay Class 2 NICs of £2.40 per week. This amount is usually paid monthly by direct debit.
2. Class 4 NIC payment of 8 per cent of your profits over £5,715. These payments are calculated in your tax return and the payment is included in the annual payments to HMRC.

HOLIDAYS

Holidays are important – not only for yourself, but also for your family. If you are completely involved with the running of the business you need time and space away from it occasionally.

When you are working from home, especially as an independent operator, two immediate problems crop up:

- It is not usually possible to have a holiday 'at home'. Your customers will not appreciate it if their calls are ignored and you will find it difficult to completely switch off.

- Your business may well depend on you financially. If you take a holiday the business will stop functioning and the income from it will be reduced.

As well as budgeting for these periods of loss of income, let your customers know in advance when you will be away and, if possible, give them a contact number in case of emergency. Ideally this should be a separate phone line with an answering service that you can access remotely.

As well as taking holidays, make sure that you organize your working life to include meetings and contacts with other business people in your local area. A lot of independent, self-employed instructors only have contact with other instructors at the local test centre. Widen your scope and get involved not only with your local instructor groups, but also with other business groups in your area.

PENSIONS

In the early days of setting up and running a business it can be difficult to put aside any money, but a personal pension plan will provide for financial security in retirement and can be a very tax-efficient and effective way of saving or investing. There are plenty of schemes available for individual sole traders, with many of them offering flexible payments, payment breaks and, in a few cases, a limited number of withdrawals.

While you are running your business you will be concentrating on making the business a success and may feel that the business does not have sufficient resources for you to spend money on a pension plan. With some businesses it is possible to sell up when it comes to retirement age, but this is not always possible or practical with a small business such as a driving school. Often, when the owner retires the business retires as well. Other factors could be involved; you may have to retire earlier than you originally planned or envisaged; the business may not make enough money for you to retire on;

and although the state retirement pension provides a basic income, it is not as much for the self-employed as it is for an employed person.

For all these reasons it makes sense to start arranging a pension scheme of some sort as early as possible. The most straightforward way to do this is to pay into a personal pension because you then get tax relief on the payments and it is therefore a very efficient and effective way of saving.

Most personal pensions have flexible arrangements. With many of them you can either invest a lump sum or make regular payments into the scheme and you should be able to alter the premiums from time to time. You can usually opt for an increasing payment and/or for a joint life pension, which means that the pension would still be paid to the remaining partner after the death of one or the other.

BOOKKEEPING AND ACCOUNTANCY

One aspect of starting their own business that seems to bother some people is the thought of having to deal with the business's accounts. A person who has been used to having income tax and National Insurance contributions deducted regularly by their employer can be put off by the prospect of having to deal with organizations like HMRC (HM Revenue and Customs). The reality is that the tax people are not as authoritarian as we are sometimes led to believe. They publish (via their website and in leaflet form) plenty of material to help the new small business and are ready to give advice where required.

Remember that 'business and pleasure do not mix'. This is particularly the case with finances.

Keep your business and personal finances completely separate. This way you will know exactly how the business stands and it should make your tax returns more straightforward to complete each year. There have been many examples over the years of instructors who have used daily income from their business as spending money and who then run into difficulties. If you do not feel completely confident about bookkeeping and running accounts, make sure you get someone to help and use your own time more profitably in the areas that you are good at.

The records you will need to run an efficient bookkeeping system include:

- cash book;
- sales record;
- purchases record;
- balance sheet;
- profit and loss forecast.

Cash book

The cash book is where you should keep a daily record of money you have been paid and any payments you have made, whether these payments are by cash, cheque or card. This record of income and expenditure can then be checked against the bank statement.

Sales record

As well as a daily cash book, it is worthwhile keeping a record of monthly sales, especially if you have customers who pay in advance or in arrears rather than on a 'per lesson' basis.

The sales record should include the customer's name, date of work done, invoice number if applicable, and date of payment.

Purchases record

Keep separate files for paid and unpaid invoices. By doing this you will be able to see exactly what the business owes at any one time. Always remember to obtain a receipt for your records for all payments you make.

These are the main records for a small, home-based business, but it may be appropriate, particularly if the business is to grow, to add a profit/loss forecast and a balance sheet to improve your understanding of the state of the business. For details of P/L forecasts and balance sheets, including examples, see Chapter 4.

There are different ways you can manage your bookkeeping, either on a paper-based manual method, or by using one of the many software programs that are available.

EMPLOYING OTHER INSTRUCTORS

Remember that if you employ other instructors, even if they regard themselves as 'self-employed', you could be liable for their income tax and National Insurance unless you can show that they are genuinely working for themselves. To make sure, you should draw up a detailed and accurate agreement setting out the terms and conditions of your arrangement with them.

6

Marketing and promoting your business

This chapter contains information on how to market your new business and make people aware of your school; how to promote and maintain effective customer awareness skills; the importance of dealing with people as individual customers and not simply 'the pupil'; pricing your lessons at an appropriate level; using the internet as a marketing tool; and the voluntary code of practice for the industry.

SALES AND MARKETING

Setting up a new driving school does not require a large sales staff or complex marketing strategies. What you do need, however, is a realistic plan of how you will persuade people to use your service rather than that of your competitors.

As a small independent business you should not need to spend large sums of money on advertising. Local newspapers, directories and radio can be expensive and often produce relatively poor results. Word of mouth and personal recommendation can be the most valuable form of advertising. Have a supply of business cards to give out to your pupils to hand on to friends, colleagues and family to generate recommendations.

Most of your potential customers will think that all driving schools are much the same, providing the same level of service. After all, in their view, 'a driving lesson is a driving lesson'. The service you provide, especially as a new business, should offer the customer something extra. To achieve this, make sure you offer some tangible elements as well as your general level of instruction:

- training programmes and course syllabus;
- learning notes and driver records;
- appointment cards;
- assessment forms;
- additional services such as 'Pass Plus' or motorway lessons.

To promote and advertise your new business, set yourself a budget and choose those marketing methods that are affordable and which will target your proposed market for a reasonable amount of time. Do not commit yourself to an advertising programme that you will not be able to finance over an extended period, or which is unrealistic in terms of your needs.

Promotional tools

- Word of mouth or recommendations. Encourage your existing customers to recommend your business to their family and friends. Consider offering special incentives for the customer and anyone they recommend.
- Business cards and leaflets. Have a supply of properly designed, eye-catching information cards or leaflets.
- Promotional cards. Use these to display on noticeboards, staff canteens, shops, etc.
- Leaflet drops. Have a professionally prepared leaflet to put through doors in your target area.
- Local newspapers and radio. Promote the business with adverts (which can be quite expensive) and/or editorial features. You will find that your local media are generally very supportive of

local small businesses – especially if you have a story or newsworthy item to give them.
- Website. Most of your potential customers will use the internet to find a particular service. Creating and maintaining a website can be more cost-effective than printed promotional material, but it needs to be done in a professional way.
- Business directories. These can be very effective, particularly for a new business, but can be rather expensive, so be realistic about what would be most effective. Check out www.yell.com and www.thomsonlocal.com for more details.
- Local magazines. It is relatively easy to identify the readership of local church, parish or student magazines and newsletters. Advertising in this type of local media is relatively inexpensive and can target your particular customer base.

Pricing

There are several factors that determine how you should price your lessons, but the main one is what the price conveys to the customer. Customers will often associate a slightly higher price with better quality; if you set your prices too low there is a danger that you will be associated with the lower end of the market and possibly an image of poor quality. You have to decide for yourself where you want to pitch your business and whether local conditions will influence or affect your pricing.

Not many people make a choice based on price alone. Although a lot of us will shop around for the best price on like-for-like items, when it comes to choosing a service most customers look for good value combined with a quality service.

Advertising

Although word of mouth is probably the most effective (and least costly!) form of advertising, there may be times – especially in the early stages – when you feel you need to use paid advertising. Any advert should be simple, memorable and should get your message over in clear terms.

Before committing large sums of money on a lengthy programme of advertising, monitor your initial adverts, for example by asking each new pupil how they heard about your business

Checklist

- word of mouth recommendations from existing customers are the most effective;
- generate good PR for yourself and your business;
- be selective with your adverts;
- make your adverts stand out;
- measure the effectiveness of any advertising programme.

Advertising outlets

Potential advertising methods include:

- local newspapers – especially if you have a particular new product or service to offer;
- phone directories – a display advert will make your business stand out, but can be relatively expensive;
- displayed cards in local shops, clubs, colleges and youth groups can generate an awareness of your school to your potential market and age groups;
- customize your car(s) with effective advertising material;
- direct drops of leaflets through letter boxes in your local catchment area – housing estates and so on.

Online marketing

Online marketing can be important. Even the smallest business should ideally have a website. A well-constructed site can affect how your prospective customers view your business and need not be too costly to set up. There is no need to include a huge amount of information just sufficient so that people know how to contact you and what you can offer.

Do not underestimate or ignore the power of the internet. No more than ten or fifteen years ago all our communications were by telephone, fax and post. Advertising would have been confined to local papers, Yellow Pages and perhaps local radio. Nowadays the internet gives you access to a much wider audience and it is possible to target your particular potential customers by effective use of websites, search engines, blogs, twitter and online forums.

Website

To set up an effective website, it needs to be clear, usable, user-friendly and easy to find. Even if you set up the most efficient and effective website, you then need to make sure that people know about you. This is normally done by what is called 'search engine optimization' (SEO). For most small businesses, particularly if you are working entirely on your own, organizing SEO can be achieved by following a few basic rules:

- Name: use a domain name that is relevant to your business (for example, joebloggsdriving.co.uk) so that a search engine can easily match the keywords.
- Text: make sure that the name of the business is included in the text as well as in the title. Ordinary text is important to the scanning and reading of sites by search engines.
- Keywords: use 'keywords' early in the main body of the text. For example, have 'driver training', 'driving instruction' and so on included in headings and in the first few paragraphs.
- Links: an effective way of improving the ranking is to link to other sites and, more importantly, encourage others to link to your site. Google, for instance, has a system whereby a site is assessed partly on the number of sites linked to you.

- Content: the text on the first page of your website should be useful to the prospective reader and informative in plain language. Any extra pages you construct should again contain some of your keywords and should be linked to the home page of the site.

Pay-per-click

If you are uncertain about setting up an effective site using the SEO rules, you might consider a pay-per-click (ppc) form of advertising. Several services including Google and Yahoo! offer ppc adverts. As the term indicates, you pay a fee to the provider each time someone 'clicks' on your site. This can be an efficient way of keeping your website higher in the rankings and can be reasonably cost-effective.

To organize your website, consider what your objectives are; for example, marketing to potential customers, contact and support for existing customers. Draw up an outline of what you want the site to include. Have a good look at competitors' and other websites for ideas. Check whether your existing internet service provider (ISP) can host the site. Register your domain name, but keep it short. When you build the site, make sure that it is search-engine optimized as above. Monitor the usage of the site and check how effective it is in achieving your original aims for it. Keep the site up to date by adding new material, particularly on the home page.

Website content

When writing the text for your business website, make sure that you emphasize the benefits to the new customer of using your particular driving school rather than another. A lot of websites and adverts for driving instructors simply list what the firm does. Although it is important to outline the main facts, most people are influenced by emotions and feelings. To achieve this, you need to include the benefits that the prospective customer will get from your particular service.

For example, the customer will always be thinking 'What's in it for me?', so include emotive phrases and expressions such as 'Pass your test easily/quickly...', ' fully structured...', ' free handouts...', 'top-grade DSA instructor...'. In other words, make sure you include the benefits to the customer and are not simply emphasizing what the school does.

Website checklist

- set up a website for your customers;
- keep it up to date, interesting and informative;
- check whether you need to use a search engine listing;
- include your website details on all stationery and any marketing material you send out.

E-mail marketing

E-mail is an effective way to reach new and existing customers without too much expense. You can build a list of e-mail addresses from all enquiries and current customers, but only if they specifically opt in. This can be done by providing a 'sign up' option on the website. Remember that you can get into difficulties by sending unsolicited e-mails.

Use your mailing list to send regular newsletters about yourself and your business and let customers know about any special offers. If the mailing list gets too big you can always use an online marketing service to manage it for you.

Public relations

Having set up your new home-based business, you need to let everyone know that you are there. Getting suitable coverage in your local press is free and can be much more powerful than paid advertising. If you can help a local journalist or broadcaster with a comment on key local issues or offer a picture story you can gain access to thousands of potential customers. Once you manage to obtain some coverage you can keep referring to it so as to retain the public awareness of your business.

To get your idea across effectively make sure the press notice is brief, snappy and to the point:

- Who is it about? Your business, who you are, what the business does, key people.
- Where is the business based?
- When and where the event happened or when it will take place.
- What happened? Be brief!
- Why did it happen? For example, a response to a survey or a new development in the industry.

Keep the press briefing to a single sheet of A4 paper and include photos if possible and if appropriate to the story. Contact details should, of course, be clearly stated.

Marketing checklist

Have you considered all or any of the following:

- Direct drops of leaflets through letter boxes in your catchment area – housing estates and so on.
- Pupil referrals. Use special offers to new customers and the current pupil.
- Local PR in newspapers and radio.
- Special offers to current pupils – post-test training, Pass Plus etc.
- Regular advertising.
- Displays at local events/shopping centres/exhibitions, etc.
- Website – online blogs/marketing.

CUSTOMER CARE AND PROFESSIONAL STANDARDS

Customers (and, more importantly, potential customers) now have a great deal of freedom of choice between suppliers – particularly in the service industry. Furthermore, their expectations of efficient service are greater than previously. Your instruction skills may be top-grade, but if you let your customers down in any way your business and your reputation will suffer.

Customer loyalty is an important factor in a one-to-one service industry such as driving instruction. Recommendation is probably by far the most effective marketing tool and is much less costly than any advertising or promotion.

As well as offering good-quality instruction, think of other areas of your business – personal appearance, punctuality and timekeeping during lessons. Avoid 'short-changing' the pupil; give a little extra rather than a little less time.

Customers' expectations include:

- *Efficiency.* Be on time for all lesson appointments. A wait of two to three minutes can seem a long time to a waiting pupil – five minutes is unacceptable.
- *Honesty.* Carry out your business and instruction honestly and professionally, but tactfully.
- *Politeness.* Maintain the instructor–pupil relationship in a friendly, but not overfamiliar, manner.
- *Respect.* The pupil can rightly expect to be treated as an individual person, and does not want to be patronized or treated dismissively.
- *Dress code.* You are not necessarily expected to wear formal clothing or a traditional business suit, but at least you should be neat, clean and tidy – whatever style of dress you choose.

Dealing with enquiries

Make sure that your telephone is answered promptly and efficiently. If you use an answer machine, try to follow up enquiries promptly. Research has shown that customers tend to expect their call to be answered within four rings of the phone. It has been shown that many people will give up after six or eight rings. Whoever answers your phone is the first point of contact for the prospective customer. Make sure that the enquiry is dealt with effectively, with clear, concise and accurate information.

Follow-up procedures

Every enquiry, however vague or imprecise, should be treated seriously and with respect. Have a system in place whereby the enquiry details can be logged for future reference, so that you can follow up the enquiry at a later date and as a memory jogger for any further contact.

Promotions and marketing

Promoting your business is essential. Potential customers need to be made aware of what your business is offering. Marketing is normally vitally important to the home-based business because of the lack of passing trade. However, as a driving instructor, your car is probably your office as well as the training vehicle. Make sure that it is clean and well presented, with clear, sensible advertising material displayed. The name and telephone number of your business must be prominent. Make sure that the service you are offering is what your potential customers would expect.

Selling your services

The most important way of selling your services is by personal recommendation from satisfied customers. A satisfied customer can be a very useful marketing tool.

Make sure that any claims you make – regarding pass rates, for example – can be substantiated. To do this you must keep accurate customer records and not rely solely on verbal claims.

You should be able to organize a system of feedback from customers. This could be done by way of a fairly uncomplicated question form to give out to customers during their course of lessons or send out to them at the end.

Promotional literature

Business cards and leaflets should set out the details of your business in clear terms. Remember that leaflets are easily discarded, so consider whether to include some form of discount to new customers on presenting the leaflet.

Any advertising that you do should be completely honest, accurate and straightforward. You should avoid any inaccurate or misleading claims relating to your qualifications or pass rates.

Customer records

At any one time you could have a large number of pupils under instruction who will all be at different stages in their learning. Even those who have reached the same stage will not have covered identical aspects of driving in exactly the same order. Your students will be of a wide range of abilities and aptitudes. All of them will have individual likes, dislikes and preferences. For teaching purposes alone, this information is vitally important in helping you to create a suitable and effective learning environment for each individual pupil.

From a business point of view you need to have a system in place that will enable you to have an up to date picture of the status of each pupil. Without some form of record keeping, it will be impossible for you to carry all of the necessary information in your head from week to week. Apart from the obvious information such as name and address, your records could usefully contain some of the following details:

- driving licence: driver number, categories covered, expiry date;
- eyesight: spectacles, contact lenses?
- theory test: application, date and time, result;
- lesson payments;
- tuition record: topics covered;
- assessment and progress report: skills and procedures;
- route record: intermediate/advanced routes (keeping a record will help to avoid unnecessary repetition);
- practical test: application, fees, date and time, result;
- Pass Plus sessions.

As well as using a 'driver's record' for each customer, it is also worthwhile having a system to record the details of each customer. This may be done manually or on a computer and may include details of payments made and lessons taken. This kind of system will be helpful in building up a profile of your customer base.

If you take money in advance for lessons, it is important that you keep an accurate record in case of queries. Similarly, if you take money for a test application, make sure that the pupil is aware of the circumstances regarding a refund.

New customers and enquiries

Your first point of contact with a new customer will normally be by telephone. Whoever answers the phone (at your home/office or on your mobile) should be able to deal with the enquiry promptly and effectively. Most efficient schools use an enquiry form to complete during the conversation. This ensures that nothing is missed out and that the customer has all the required information. This document should cover all the essential information such as the customer's name, telephone numbers, address and other details including availability and possible start date for training.

As well as the enquiry form for completion make sure you have the basic items of equipment – pen, pad, diary and calendar – available and be prepared to supply accurate and up to date information about licences, test fees and DSA contact details. Remember that this first point of contact is the most important and may make the difference between getting a new customer who is likely to spend considerable sums of money with you, or alternatively a lost opportunity!

Be professional, but at the same time be friendly and approachable.

Telephone enquiry checklist

- Introduce yourself and the school.
- Location – is the pupil in your normal pick-up area?
- Next available date you can take on a new pupil.
- What days and times will the pupil be available?
- Does the customer know about your prices?
- Pupil's name, home address, telephone number, mobile number.
- Pupil's previous driving experience.
- Date and time of first lesson.
- Licence – bring both parts to first lesson.
- Eyesight – does the pupil wear spectacles or use contact lenses?
- Pick-up point (if different to home address).
- Any questions from the pupil?
- How did the pupil hear about the school?
- Reminders:
    - 'See you on…'
    - 'Bring your licence…'
    - 'Any problems about the booking, please let us know as soon as possible'.

Follow-ups

As soon as possible after the initial enquiry the new customer should be given full details about your school. Ideally, this would be done by personal delivery, but at least by first class post the same day. If the customer has made a booking the information should include details of the first appointment and reminders about producing both parts of their provisional driving licence and that an eyesight test will need to be carried out on the first lesson.

First lesson

On all lessons, but most importantly on a first lesson with a new pupil, make sure you are punctual. A late arrival is not conducive to professionalism and to your reputation as an efficient instructor. On the other hand do not arrive too early as this can be very off-putting for someone who is not ready and who is probably nervous about the first meeting.

Full details of how to conduct a lesson and up to date instruction/coaching methods are included in *The Driving Instructor's Handbook* and *Practical Teaching Skills for Driving Instructors*, but a brief overview of best practice and procedures on a first lesson includes:

- Before the lesson (or before starting your instruction) check with the pupil whether they have had any previous driving experience and whether they have taken (or applied for) the theory test. Be careful about the responses – some pupils might not like to say that they have driven previously, while others will inadvertently have an overoptimistic idea of the amount and type of driving they have already done.
- The pupil should be made fully aware of the procedures for the theory and practical tests, and the need for thorough preparation for both parts. At this stage, you can emphasize that there are various CDs and books that they can use to enhance the learning process.

- Find out from the pupil if they are likely to be able to have private driving practice, but do not press the point or make them feel that it is essential if there is any hesitancy about it on their part.

As indicated above, on the first lesson, check the provisional licence details and make sure that the pupil can read a registration plate from the required distance.

If the pupil genuinely has no previous driving experience you will need to drive to an appropriate training area. Use this time to establish a working relationship with the pupil, but avoid any temptation to show off your own driving skills. Emphasize that this lesson will include an essential element of explanation and discussion, but that they will get to drive the car at some point during the lesson.

Note that this 'first lesson' description is intended to be an overview of the professional standards to be implemented. Full details of instructional methods and lesson construction are in *The Driving Instructor's Handbook* and *Practical Teaching Skills for Driving Instructors*.

Documentation

As well as keeping accurate records for your business accounts, it is important to have a system of recording and maintaining a proper record of pupil's progress. This can take the form of a 'Driver's record' as suggested by the DSA or a fully professional system such as that offered by Driving School Pro (web: www.drivingschoolpro.co.uk; tel: 01305 834677). With either system, the pupil has a detailed analysis of their training schedule to take away at the end of each lesson.

Private practice

The DSA's official advice to L drivers is that they should have professional instruction with an ADI, supported by plenty of private practice. This practice can be beneficial as long as it is done at the right time and in a structured way.

At an early stage in the pupil's training you will need to establish whether this is possible and if so what type of car they will be using and who will be supervising the practice. Right from the start establish with the pupil that you will recommend when to start the private practice so as to avoid the situation where the pupil (and the supervising driver!) gets into difficult and potentially dangerous situations too early in their training.

Dress code

As part of your professionalism a sensible and appropriate dress code is essential. Clearly, a jacket and tie approach is not usually necessary, but an untidy, sloppy appearance or clothes or footwear that are *too* casual will give an unprofessional impression.

Clothes can be 'smart casual' and should be clean and tidy, with comfortable, but appropriate footwear. Similarly, personal cleanliness and hygiene are important in creating the right professional image – especially as you will be spending longish periods of time with the customer in a relatively confined space.

In this respect, make sure you allow time during the working day for a shower and/or a change of shirt, particularly in hot weather. You should be able to present the same professional image and appearance in the last lesson as at the start of your working day. In the same way, your personal hygiene should include an awareness of body odours and bad breath – especially if you are a smoker. But remember that smoking in the tuition car is not allowed by law.

The car

Keep the instruction car clean and tidy, both outside and in. Open the windows as often as possible, particularly between lessons to avoid a build-up of unpleasant or stale odours. Keep the steering wheel, handbrake and gear lever clean by using wet wipes between lessons.

Conversation

Always be careful in your conversations with pupils. Comments and opinions can be misconstrued, particularly if they are relayed to someone else out of context. Clearly, the use of 'dubious' language, innuendo or slightly suggestive stories that could be misinterpreted are not part of the professional instructor's approach.

Personal contact

Avoid physical contact with the pupil whenever possible, including times when you or the pupil are buckling or unbuckling the seat belt and when using the gear lever or handbrake. There will be the occasional time when contact is made accidentally, for example when making a steering correction, but avoid contact if possible. For example, when meeting the pupil, saying goodbye or congratulating after passing the test, a brief handshake is perfectly acceptable, but nothing more!

Customer care checklist

Most self-employed, independent instructors who have been successful over a period of time generally agree that the list of important features that set them apart from the 'run of the mill' or 'cheapy' schools includes:

- Making sure that the business phone is answered promptly and effectively by someone who knows about the business and who can deal with enquiries and bookings efficiently.
- Following up all leads and enquiries straightaway and providing the customer with up to date information about the school and its methods.
- Trying to avoid expensive and ineffective advertising by using existing customers' recommendations and word of mouth.
- Having a professional, but friendly, approach to all customers. Remember that the most important person in the car is the

customer and that they are all individual, with individual aspirations and expectations.

- Keeping the car up to date, clean and tidy.
- Presenting a clean, smart and approachable personal image.
- Using effective training aids and providing a record of the pupil's progress.
- Being efficient with timekeeping, lessons and punctuality.
- Keeping effective business records and monitoring them accurately and regularly.
- Keeping up to date with DSA information and best practices for teaching/learning/coaching methods.

HANDLING COMPLAINTS

Complaints from customers can be dealt with in a positive manner. The important issue is to try to ensure that any minor problems are tackled before they become major problems.

Your complaints procedure should be clear; stating that in the first instance clients should approach you with their grievance. If you cannot come to an amicable agreement, clients should be advised to refer to the DSA to consider and advise on the matter. In some circumstances the Registrar of ADIs is prepared to offer advice in an attempt to resolve disputes between instructor and pupil.

The industry has a voluntary code of practice (see page 142) that deals with this subject. You – or your franchisor – should have an effective procedure in place for dealing with complaints. Dealing with complaints properly and fairly can help to maintain good customer relations. The important thing, though, is to try to deal with minor queries before they turn into complaints.

PERSONAL CUSTOMER SERVICE

Good and efficient customer service is a key issue in running a small business and can be vital in ensuring its success over a period of years. A lot of people in new businesses, and particularly in driver training, make the mistake of thinking that price is all-important to the customer, but this is not the case. Goodwill and personal customer service are big factors and can make a significant difference. As a small business or a local franchise you have an advantage over the bigger companies and you should be able to exploit this advantage by offering a top-quality individual service to your customers.

The key point to bear in mind is that this type of service is mainly about building a good working relationship with each and every customer and treating them as individuals.

Follow a few basic rules to get your customer services technique up to the standard you need:

- The customer is always right. Most people will be ready to talk about unsatisfactory service they receive, but do not normally mention average service. Make sure your standard of service is exceptional.
- Go the extra mile. In a small business you can usually offer a service over and above what the customer might expect. Try to fulfil any customer requests that are not necessarily part of what you normally offer. In this way you will have a distinct advantage over larger firms who will only offer a standard service.
- Show the customer that you care. Take an individual interest in each customer. Respond as soon as possible to enquiries; follow up with a personal call; be punctual; don't 'short time' the pupil – in fact, try to add a little extra from time to time.
- Be available. As a small business you need to make yourself (or at least someone in your business) available outside normal working hours. Respond quickly and promptly to telephone, texts or e-mail messages. Customers will expect this level of service and will be disappointed with any delay.

- Problems: Follow up as early as possible if a pupil misses an appointment without any explanation. Anyone who is not completely happy with the service you offer will tend to walk away rather than complain or have any kind of confrontation. If something has gone wrong try to find out exactly what the problem is. Whether you succeed in solving the problem or not the customer will almost certainly remember you for the attempt you made rather than the original problem. If it looks as if you have 'got it wrong', say so! Accept that, occasionally, things will go wrong; mistakes can be made and misunderstandings can arise. In this situation make an apology to the customer and offer them something extra.
- Pricing and service. Do not confuse these two important items. Customers will judge each of them quite independently. Even if you deliver low-cost lessons or have any special offers and discounts the expectation is still that an appropriate level of service will be given. Good value (rather than cheap) combined with excellent personal service is usually the most effective.

CODE OF PRACTICE

The DSA and the main ADI consultative organizations have produced a code of practice that places emphasis on professional standards and business ethics. Once you have qualified, you will be expected to operate within this framework. Some of the main criteria are detailed in the following sections.

Personal conduct

You should:

- behave in a professional manner towards clients;
- treat your clients with respect and consideration;
- be polite, punctual and presentable;

- avoid physical contact with clients, except in emergencies or in the normal course of greeting;
- give value for money;
- not discuss with other people any matters that a pupil has disclosed;
- avoid acting in any way that contravenes legislation on discrimination.

Your training vehicle should be:

- properly maintained;
- safe and roadworthy;
- legal for giving instruction;
- clean, both internally and externally.

Business dealings

You should:

- Safeguard and account for any monies paid in advance for driving lessons, test fees or any other purpose. These details should be available to clients on request.
- Provide clients, on or before their first lesson, with a written copy of your terms of business. This should include:
    - the legal identity of your school, together with a full address and telephone number at which you or your representative can be contacted;
    - the price and duration of lessons;
    - the price and conditions for using the school car for driving tests;
    - the terms under which cancellation by either party may take place; and
    - a complaints procedure.

- Make sure clients are entitled to drive your vehicle, have a valid driving licence and can read a number plate from the prescribed distance. Ensure also that when presenting them for driving tests they have all the necessary documentation and your car is roadworthy.
- Forecast clients' readiness, and advise them when to apply for their theory and practical tests, taking into account local waiting times. Do not cancel or rearrange tests without clients' agreement. If you decide to withhold the use of your vehicle for a test, clients should be given sufficient notice to avoid their loss of the test fee.
- Make sure that any pupils who are taking an intensive course of lessons are aware of the potential loss of fees if the test is not taken or if the course is not completed.
- Devote *all* of the lesson time to the pupil's instruction, not to your own personal business.
- At all times do your best to teach clients correct driving skills according to the DSA's recommended syllabus.

Advertising

Your advertising should be honest. Any claims you make should be capable of verification and comply with the codes of practice set down by the Advertising Standards Authority. Any advertising referring to pass rates should not be open to misinterpretation, and the basis on which you calculate the pass rates should be made clear.

After passing all three exams, when you register as an ADI you will be sent a leaflet containing full details of the code of practice. If you are already qualified, copies are available from the DSA in Nottingham (for contact details see page 217).

7

Driving licences and driving tests

This chapter contains information on all aspects of the driving licence and driving test, including how to apply, the costs involved, and a summary of the requirements for each part of the driving test.

DRIVING LICENCES

Driving licences were first introduced in the UK in 1904. At that time, and for many years afterwards, they were issued by local council offices and were normally renewable each year. An annual licence at that time was five shillings (the equivalent of 25p in today's money!).

By the late 1960s there was an obvious need for a more structured, centralized system of driver licensing and the Driver and Vehicle Licence Centre at Swansea was subsequently opened. At that stage regional offices of the Department of Transport continued to issue licences for commercial vehicle drivers. Since then various changes have taken place, and now all driving licences – including vocational licences for lorry and bus drivers – are dealt with by the Driver and Vehicle Licensing Agency (DVLA) as it is now known.

Only photo-card licences are now issued by DVLA, with the old-style paper licences being phased out.

The licence shows details of all categories for which the driver has entitlement, including lorries and buses. Any provisional entitlement is shown, together with any relevant restrictions such as maximum trailer weights or 'not for hire or reward'.

Whereas a paper licence normally has an extended expiry date (usually to age 70), the photo-card licence has to be renewed after 10 years to keep the photographic likeness up to date.

A fact sheet on photo-card licences (INF61) is available from DVLA by telephoning the automated service on 01 792 792 792 or by visiting the DVLA website at www.dvla.gov.uk.

PROVISIONAL LICENCE

To start driving on the public roads your pupils will need to obtain a provisional licence. They can apply in advance for the licence, but must not drive until they receive the licence. On receipt, the licence should be checked for accuracy and the DVLA should be notified if there are any errors. The licence is in two parts – the photo card that shows which vehicles the person is entitled to drive, and the counterpart that shows other details such as any endorsements or restrictions. Remember – if there is a need to produce the licence for any reason both parts are required. It's worth keeping a note of the licence details – particularly the 'driver number' – or a photocopy, in case the original is lost or mislaid.

You need to make sure that the pupil's eyesight is up to the legal standard. For car driving, the requirement is to be able to read, in good daylight, a car number plate from a distance of 20 metres (for the new-style, eight-digit plates) and at 20.5 metres for the older, seven-digit plates. Spectacles or other lenses can be worn for the test, but they should then always be worn when driving.

MINIMUM AGE FOR DRIVING

The minimum age for driving a car is usually 17. Before that age the only motorized vehicle that can be driven is a moped – which is like a small motorcycle with an engine size of less than 50 cc and with a restricted speed. If you need more details about riding mopeds and motorbikes you should have a look at *Riding motorcycles* from the DSA.

Under certain circumstances a car may be driven at 16 if the driver is receiving a Disability Living Allowance at the higher rate. Other than that the new driver has to wait until his or her 17th birthday. In some European countries the minimum driving age is 18 and there have been rumours that the UK may follow suit at some time. However, there are no immediate plans for this to happen – and even if the UK law changed it would take several years to make the transition.

APPLICATION FORMS

Application forms can be obtained from most Post Offices. There are two forms that will be needed – the D1, which is the licence application, and the D750, which is for the photo-card application. Alternatively, the forms can be downloaded from www.direct.gov. uk.

When the forms are collected it is worthwhile getting the information leaflet D100. This is a very informative booklet produced by DVLA. It covers all the essential information about vehicle types and licence entitlements.

For the initial application for a first provisional licence the DVLA will require a photo and proof of identity. This would usually be a passport or birth certificate. Whichever document is used, it is worth keeping a photocopy of them, or at least making a note of the details – just in case the original is mislaid.

If a document other than your passport is sent the photograph must be validated and countersigned by a 'responsible person'. This should be someone who has known the applicant for at least two years, and who is not a relative.

To avoid the need to send important documents to DVLA, with the risk that there might be some delay in returning them or the possibility that they may get mislaid, the Post Office offer a checking service. The additional fee is currently £4, but the service is not available at all Post Offices. After checking the application the Post Office will send the forms to DVLA and return your documents to you straightaway.

The Driver and Vehicle Licensing Authority can be contacted at:

Customer Enquiries (Drivers)
DVLA
SWANSEA SA6 7JL
Tel: 0870 240 0009.
Fax: 01792 783071.
Web: www.direct.gov.uk.
E-mail: drivers.dvla@gtnet.gov.uk.

PROVISIONAL LICENCE ENTITLEMENT

A provisional licence covers the driver for cars and small passenger-carrying vehicles with up to eight passenger seats and for light goods vehicles up to 3,500 kgs gross weight.

The driver is not allowed to tow a trailer while learning.

As a provisional licence holder, L plates (or D plates in Wales) must be displayed on the front and rear of the vehicle.

An 'accompanying driver' must be over 21 and must have held a full licence for at least three years for the type of vehicle being driven.

RIDING A MOTORCYCLE OR MOPED

A full car licence usually acts as a provisional licence for motorcycles and as a full licence for mopeds. A new provisional motorcycle licence is valid for a maximum of two years. If a full licence is not obtained during that time, the licence cannot be renewed for a period of one year. The provisional licence entitles the rider to use a solo motorcycle with an engine capacity of up to 125 cc (subject to the requirements of Compulsory Basic Training). Pilllion passengers are not allowed to accompany a learner rider, even if the passenger holds a full licence for that type of machine.

Compulsory Basic Training (CBT)

The provisional licence is normally valid for riding motorcycles and mopeds on L plates. However, a Compulsory Basic Training course must be successfully completed before riding on public roads. CBT certificates are valid for two years. A separate motorcycle theory test and a practical test must be taken within the two-year period.

The CBT Certificate is required for all riders of mopeds and motorcycles. The learner has to undergo a short course of off- and on-road training before riding unaccompanied on public roads. On successful completion of the course, the learner is issued with a certificate that validates the provisional licence. This applies to anyone riding a motorcycle or moped on L plates, irrespective of when their licence was issued, and includes full category B (car licence) holders who have not passed a motorcycle test.

After taking CBT the learner may ride a machine of up to 125 cc (cubic centimetres) with a maximum power output of 11 kw (kilowatts). L plates must be displayed.

CBT certificates are valid for two years. To obtain a full licence, both the theory and practical tests have to be passed within the two-year period.

A moped is any two-wheel vehicle with an engine capacity of less than 50 cc and with a maximum speed of 30 mph (miles per hour). A moped can be ridden on L plates at 16 (provided the CBT has been completed).

Motorcycle licence categories

Category A1: light motorcycle – not exceeding 125 cc and with a maximum power output of 11 kw. This type of licence can be obtained by taking the motorcycle test on a motorcycle with an engine capacity of more than 75 cc and less than 125 cc.

Category A: standard motorcycle. The test must be taken on a bike of more than 120 cc that is capable of at least 100 kph (kilometres per hour). For the first two years the rider is restricted to a bike of up to 25 kw unless he or she takes the Direct Access route to obtaining the licence. This entails a specified training course with a specially qualified instructor.

DRIVING LICENCE FEES

The cost of a first provisional licence is currently (March 2009) £50. The Premium Service (at some Post Offices and DVLA Local Offices) is an extra £4.

The fee for a replacement – for example, for a lost or stolen licence – is £19. There is no charge for replacing the licence because of a change of name or address.

After passing the driving test there is no extra fee for the first full licence.

A photo-card licence must be renewed every 10 years so that the photo is still a reasonably true likeness.

If a licence is stolen or if it is mislaid, the DVLA must be notified. A duplicate licence costs £19.

Should the original licence subsequently be found the DVLA must be contacted straightaway. It's obviously more helpful to DVLA, and quicker, if complete details of the original licence can be given.

If the licence is needed urgently – for a test, for example – there is a system whereby DVLA can confirm the licence details direct to the examiner or the DSA.

VOCATIONAL LICENCES

A full licence for category B vehicles – cars and vans – covers the driver for goods vehicles up to 3,500 kgs gross weight and for passenger vehicles with up to nine seats. For any vehicles over those limits, or for towing large trailers, a separate licence entitlement is required.

DRIVING TESTS

Theory and hazard perception tests

The full theory test can either be booked online, at www.direct.gov.uk/booktheorytest or it can be booked by phone on 0870 0101 372. The booking offices are open Monday to Friday from 8 am to 6 pm.

Instructors can register with the DSA for a 'trainer booking' system whereby the ADIs can block book the tests they require.

You can, if you prefer, book by post by completing an application form and sending it to: The Driving Standards Agency, PO Box 148, Salford M5 3SY.

The forms are available from any driving test centre or theory test centre. To pay for the test in this way a cheque or postal order will need to be sent.

THE THEORY TEST

There are 156 theory test centres at various locations around the United Kingdom. The centres are usually located so that they are readily accessible by public transport and the test can be taken at the most convenient centre.

To find details of your local centres, go to www.dsa.gov.uk and follow the 'learning to drive' link, or phone the DSA on 0300 200 1122.

The current fee (March 2010) is £31, but check with the DSA for up to date information, as the fees are changed fairly regularly. If the booking is made by phone or online, payment can be made by credit/debit card. If an application form is used a cheque or postal order will need to be sent.

Theory Test syllabus

The theory test is computer-based and is in two parts; a multiple-choice question paper, followed by a screen-based hazard perception test. All the questions are taken from the official DSA books – *The Highway Code*, *Know your Traffic Signs* and *The Official DSA Guide to Driving – the essential skills*.

The main topic headings include:

- alertness and attention when you're driving;
- your attitude towards other road users;
- safety and your vehicle;
- safety margins and how they can be affected by different weather and road conditions;
- judgement and hazard perception;
- dealing with vulnerable road users;
- dealing with different types of vehicles;
- handling of your vehicle in different conditions;
- motorway rules;
- rules of the road;
- road and traffic signs;
- documents needed for drivers and their vehicles;
- what to do in the event of an accident;
- safety of loads.

The theory test consists of 50 multiple-choice questions to answer in a maximum of 57 minutes. The pass mark is currently 43 out of a possible 50.

Hazard Perception

The second part of the theory test involves 'hazard perception' where the candidate is presented with moving traffic situations on a computer screen. It's best if the pupil has had some practical driving experience as well as theory training before attempting the test. Remember that the theory test must be taken and passed before applying for the practical driving test – and there is usually a lengthy waiting period for that part.

The hazard perception section of the test consists of a set of video clips featuring various types of developing traffic hazards. The candidate has to respond to each hazard by clicking on the computer mouse as the hazard develops.

There are 14 different video clips with one hazard in most, but with two hazards in one clip. A maximum of five points can be scored by 'spotting' the hazard as early as possible in each clip. A late or delayed response means that a lower score would be achieved.

The hazards depicted are those that would require a response from the driver, such as changing speed or direction or by taking some other form of action.

The pass mark for this part of the test is currently 44 out of a possible 75, but the DSA constantly review the results and may adjust the minimum requirement from time to time.

This part of the test lasts about 20 minutes.

The result is usually available at the test centre within about half an hour of finishing the test.

To prepare for the theory test the pupil needs to study:

- *The Highway Code*;
- *The Official DSA Guide to Driving – the essential skills*;
- *The Official Guide to Learning to Drive*;
- *The Official Theory Test for Car Drivers*;
- *Know your Traffic Signs*.

There are also several CDs and DVDs on the market including *The Official DSA Complete Theory Test Kit* and *The Official DSA Guide to Hazard Perception DVD*.

These are useful for pupils preparing for both parts of the theory test.

A mock test for the multiple-choice test can be taken online at www.driving-tests.co.uk.

As well as the official DSA publications mentioned earlier, there are many other books, CDs and videos available. Check your local bookshops and visit your library. You'll find that there are several products from the AA, BSM and others. Choose those that seem most appropriate for your particular situation.

Special needs

If the candidate has dyslexia or reading difficulties a voiceover can be arranged. To do this the application must be supported with a letter from a doctor, teacher or some other responsible person. Extra time is allowed for the test.

Special arrangements can be made for someone who would have difficulty in using a computer mouse button.

For candidates with hearing difficulties the introductions to both parts of the test can be given by sign language.

Candidates who do not understand English can listen through a headset to the test being read in one of 20 other languages. There is no extra charge.

If the test is not available in a particular language, a translator can be used. The translator must be approved by the DSA. Arrangements for using a translator must be made at the time of booking the test. The translator's services must be booked and paid for by the candidate. Tests with translators can be arranged at a limited number of test centres.

Cancellations

If the test has to be cancelled or postponed the DSA must receive at least three clear working days' notice or the fee will be lost.

'Three days' means, for example, that the booking office would need to be contacted on the previous Wednesday for a test on the following Tuesday – and earlier if there is a Bank Holiday.

This rule is only waived in certain very exceptional circumstances.

After the test

As soon as the pupil has passed the theory test he or she can apply for the practical driving test. Make sure that you check with the DSA about the application, because they will know about possible waiting times in your area.

If the pupil fails the theory test an application for a retest can be made straightaway, but there must be at least three clear working days before actually taking the next test.

Theory test centres

As there are more than 150 theory test centres throughout England, Scotland and Wales, and six in Northern Ireland, most people have a test centre within 20 miles of their home, but this will vary depending on population densities.

THE PRACTICAL TEST

Application

Probably the most effective way to book the practical test is online at www.direct.gov.uk/bookpracticaltest. Details of the driving licence and the theory test pass certificate need to be given. Payment can be made by credit or debit card.

The test can also be booked by phone using a debit or credit card. By booking in this way you can discuss with the booking clerk a suitable time and date for you and the pupil.

When making the telephone call you will need to have the pupil's theory test pass certificate number and driving licence details. If you are using someone else's credit or debit card the cardholder must be present. The DSA booking office telephone number is 0300 200 1122. The booking clerk will need to know:

- what type of test is to be taken;
- the preferred test centre;
- available dates and times;
- personal details such as address and telephone number;
- whether the candidate has any special needs;
- if a test can be accepted at short notice.

Confirmation of the agreed date will be sent by post within a week or so.

If it is not possible to book by phone you can apply by post. Forms are available from any test centre.

The form and fee should be sent to:

Driving Standards Agency
PO Box 280
Newcastle upon Tyne
NE99 1FP

Test centres

The test can be taken at whichever test centre is most convenient for you and/or the pupil.

If the test is taken in Wales the candidate can ask for it to be conducted in Welsh.

The standard of driving required is pretty much the same throughout the UK, so most people take their test at the nearest centre to them or their instructor.

Test fees

The application fee for a practical test is currently (March 2010) £62, or £75 for an evening or weekend test.

If you book by phone you can pay by credit or debit card – VISA, Mastercard, Switch or Delta.

For an application by post you should send a cheque or postal order.

Test syllabus

The practical test includes the following main topics:

- main controls of the car;
- moving away and stopping;
- reversing to the left or right;
- turn in the road;
- reverse parking;
- emergency stop;
- use of mirrors;
- giving appropriate signals;
- use of speed;
- following distances;

- maintaining progress;
- junctions;
- judgement in overtaking, meeting and crossing other traffic;
- positioning in normal driving;
- lane discipline;
- clearance for obstructions;
- pedestrian crossings;
- position for normal stops;
- awareness and planning;
- use of ancillary controls.

Driving test examiners

The driving test examiners are all DSA-trained staff who work to a consistent standard throughout the UK.

They are regularly supervised, both by their local senior examiner and by an area supervisor who travels in the back of the car on the test. When this happens remember that the supervisor is checking on the examiner and not on the candidate's driving.

Test format

The test starts with the eyesight test. The candidate must be able to read a car number plate from 20 metres (66 feet). For the older style plates with slightly larger letters and numbers the distance is 20.5 metres (67 feet). Spectacles or contact lenses may be worn for the eyesight test, but they must then be kept on for the practical driving part of the test.

The examiner will then ask a few questions about car safety checks. These questions might require pupils to demonstrate various 'under the bonnet' checks, so make sure that they are familiar with engine oil levels, coolants, wipers and washers on your particular vehicle. They should also know about tyre safety, brake lights and indicators.

The questions usually involve either 'show me' or 'tell me' as in the following examples:

> 'Would you show me how you would check that the power steering is working properly?'
>
> 'Identify where you would check the engine oil level and explain how you would ensure that the vehicle has sufficient oil.'

In answering these questions, the candidate is not expected to physically check the fluid levels or to touch a hot engine, but may be required to open the bonnet to show the location of the various items.

The main part of the test consists of driving along a route that has been preselected by the examiner. Routes are designed to involve a wide variety of different types of road and traffic conditions including dual carriageways where this is possible.

The examiner will give clear instructions in good time about route directions. For example:

> 'Would you take the next road on the left?'
>
> 'At the end of the road I would like you to turn right.'
>
> 'Please take the second road to the left – this being the first.'
>
> 'At the roundabout I'd like you take the Brighton road – that is the third exit.'

If the wrong direction is taken it will not count as a driving error as long as the driving is correct. If the examiner gives no instruction about direction – at a crossroads, or where there are specific road markings, the pupil should follow the road, or the lane, for going ahead.

During the test there are several specified manoeuvres and exercises to be carried out, including:

- emergency stop;
- left or right reverse;
- reverse park;
- turn in the road;
- uphill and downhill start.

Some of the exercises or manoeuvres will take place at carefully selected places on the test route, while others may be done in the test centre car park at the start or end of the test.

The test usually lasts about 40 minutes or so, but this can vary, depending on the traffic conditions. Tests are run to a very tight schedule, with each examiner conducting at least seven tests a day at intervals of 57 minutes, so you and the pupil need to arrive at the test centre in good time. If you don't, the test may not take place and the fee would be lost.

To pass the test the pupil must not make any 'serious' or 'dangerous' errors. As well as this only a maximum of 15 'driving' errors are allowed.

On the day of the test the pupil needs to have the theory test certificate and both parts of their driving licence with them.

If the pupil has one of the old-style paper licences, he or she will need to take some form of visual identity such as a passport.

After the test

At the end of the test the examiner will give the successful candidate a copy of the *Driving Test Report* and will offer some guidance on it. The pupil is also issued with a *Certificate of Competence to Drive* (D10). This is the document that allows the driver to drive unaccompanied and without L plates.

If the pupil has a photo-card licence that was issued after 1 March 2004 the examiner will offer to have the full licence issued automatically. In this case, the licence will be sent by DVLA within about three weeks. In the meantime, the pupil will have the pass certificate showing entitlement to drive.

If the automatic service is not used, an application for the full licence should be made as soon as possible and in any case within two years. If not, the D10 will become invalid.

When sending off for a full licence, keep a note (or preferably a photocopy) of any documents that have been sent to DVLA.

If the pupil fails, it will be because he or she had more than 15 'driving' errors or at least one 'serious' or 'dangerous' fault. They will be given a copy of the *Test Report* showing the items that they were weak on. The examiner will offer a detailed verbal report on the reasons for the failure and an explanation of the test report. It is normal for the instructor to sit in on this part of the test.

An application for a retest can be made straightaway, but the test must not be taken within 10 working days.

Cancellations

If the test has to be cancelled or postponed the DSA must be notified at least three clear working days beforehand. In effect this means at least a week before the test, and more if there are any intervening Bank Holidays. If this is not done, the test fee will be lost and another application must be made.

The only exceptions to this rule are in the event of something serious such as a sudden illness or a family bereavement.

8

L driver training – frequently asked questions

Prospective pupils and their parents will often ask for information about a range of subjects related to the complete process of learning to drive and obtaining a full licence.

This chapter guides you through the procedures with information and suggested answers on most of these queries.

PRE-DRIVER TRAINING

What is 'pre-driver' training?

Pre-driver training is usually for pupils under the age of 17, enabling them to start on their driver training before reaching the minimum legal age for obtaining a licence to drive on the road. The practical training is usually carried out at special 'off-road' centres under the supervision of qualified instructors. This means that you can simulate normal driving situations for the pupil, but in a totally traffic-free environment.

This type of learning can also be useful for more mature novice drivers – especially those who are very nervous about the prospect of driving on the roads for the first time. Using an off-road facility means that the pupil is more likely to gain confidence in handling the vehicle without the pressures of faster-moving traffic around them.

Several local authorities and individual schools offer a variation of 'pre-driver' courses that sometimes consist only of 'in class' theory sessions. These programmes are good in providing a basis in driver education, but you can point out and emphasize that there is no substitute for effective 'hands on' practical training with a professional instructor with a link to the theory.

What are the advantages?

The main advantage of pre-driver training is that pupils are able to learn the basic control skills and safe driving procedures without the worry and distraction of other traffic around them. Particularly if the course is professionally structured they will probably become more effective and safer drivers in a shorter period of time when they get on the road at 17.

In a normal course of pre-driver training you should be able to cover most of the following syllabus topics:

- safe vehicle checks;
- starting, stopping, steering;
- effective braking, stopping exercises;
- use of mirrors, blind spots;
- effective use of MSM;
- approach to simulated hazards;
- reversing and parking exercises.

This type of programme should provide your pupils with a good grounding so that these skills and routines become second nature when they start their driving on public roads.

How can I organize pre-driver training?

You might find that your local education authority (or an individual school) runs some form of training, which you may be able to link into. If not, a club or youth group in your area may be interested in having a course organized for them – possibly in conjunction with other instructors in your area. You can usually find details about pre-driver training courses in your area by contacting your local authority road safety department.

What if I am not able to offer pre-driver courses?

Training courses are available at various centres around the UK.

The cost of training varies enormously, depending on whether it is a subsidized course with the local authority; a commercially based course with one of the national organizations; or individual lessons with a local instructor. You might find that you have to sign up for a complete programme of training for, say, a complete term, or you might be able to buy the instruction by the hour.

A typical programme offers a mix of theory and practical training for small groups of pupils at about £100 for a half day. Individual driving lessons are currently about £20 per hour.

Are there any disadvantages?

The only disadvantage of off-road, pre-driver training is that sometimes you will find that courses run by non-professionals are unstructured and lacking in real objectives. This can happen with courses run by volunteer groups or organized by someone who is not familiar with the syllabus requirements. It can lead to a situation where the pupil becomes fairly proficient with the basic car control skills, but is lacking in any real understanding of the important safety procedures that are needed in preparation for driving on the road with other traffic. If pupils do not have training in these basics – proper observations, awareness, system of control, MSM routines – they will undoubtedly struggle when confronted by fast-moving traffic around them.

It's important, therefore, that the course is a properly structured professional training programme, with an appropriate mixture of theory and practical elements.

Is there a minimum age limit?

The normal age for starting this type of training is around 15 to 16 years. Under that age there is not a lot of point because the pupil is going to have to wait much longer before driving on the road.

Some courses allow pupils to enrol at an earlier age, with the stipulation that they must be over a particular height (so that the foot controls can be operated effectively). This is fine as long as it is not treated just as a 'fun' exercise and that the training is continued closer to the pupil's 17th birthday.

With some instructors and schools the minimum age is about 15 to 15 and a half years because of insurance limitations. Make sure that you are properly insured for this type of activity, particularly if you decide to offer off-road instruction or practice for groups or individuals.

Is a driving licence needed?

Pupils would not normally need a driving licence for off-road instruction as long as the driving takes place on a completely private area.

If you offer off-road courses or individual lessons make sure that the proposed training area *is* completely private because if this is not the case the pupil will need a driving licence and to be adequately covered by insurance. For example, if you are using an area 'to which the public normally have access' – such as some parts of school grounds – you may need to close off the training area to restrict access for other users.

Does the pupil have to belong to a group?

Pre-driver training can be arranged individually as well as in groups. You could check with your local council or education authority to see if they already run any courses in your area before you start to organize your own programme. If so, it might be an advantage for you to offer your services to supplement their programme.

There are a few advantages in pupils taking their training as part of a group. They can learn from each other's driving, and it is often more effective for you to explain the basic controls and procedures to a small group than individually.

Individual hourly paid instruction can often be arranged, but this would normally be a little more expensive than group instruction – especially if it's subsidized by the local authority.

Can a friend or relative provide off-road pre-driver training?

Yes, if they can find an appropriate training area that is safe and completely private. They would need to make absolutely sure that they are adequately covered by insurance. There have been several reported incidents where someone has damaged their car in these circumstances and then found that the insurance company will not cover the cost – sometimes because of age and sometimes because of the 'off-road' element. Most motor insurance policies are for cover on public roads.

However, it's much more effective for pupils to learn with a properly qualified professional instructor. They then won't have any problems with insurance, and are more likely to learn in a controlled and structured way.

Will the pupil need special insurance to learn with friends or family?

As previously indicated, if the pupil is learning with a qualified instructor or as part of an official group the instructor or course organizer will deal with any insurance matters. As well as motor insurance, they will (or should) have public liability cover. If pupils organize their own training, they should check with their insurance company or agent.

STRUCTURING YOUR PUPILS' TRAINING

How should lessons be structured?

Lessons with a qualified instructor should be properly structured and would normally follow the DSA official syllabus for learning to drive, but adapted to suit the particular needs, ability and aptitude of individual pupils. Full details of the syllabus are given in *The Official DSA Guide to Driving – the essential skills*, a DSA book published by The Stationery Office.

Driving is one of those jobs that involves many complex interrelated tasks and skills. It takes quite a lot of time and effort to reach a reasonable standard of proficiency. Probably none of us will ever quite master the complete range of skills – there's no such thing as a 'perfect driver'.

There is little point in the pupil attempting to take the practical driving test until both pupil and instructor are confident about the pupil's ability. The DSA have suggested that up to 50 per cent of all driving test candidates are not even capable of carrying out the basic driving skills.

The theory test must be taken and passed before your pupil can apply for the practical part. There is, of course, a delay of several weeks for the test in most areas, so you should allow for this when planning the programme of lessons. You will need to take into account any private practice the pupil might be having.

To help with planning and logging the pupil's progress within the syllabus the DSA have produced a 'Driver's Record' that is completed in stages during the learning process.

How frequently should lessons be taken?

Everyone learns at a different rate and in various ways, so there is no precise answer. It's generally agreed, though, that lessons should be taken at regular intervals – especially in the early stages. There's a lot of information for the pupil to take in at that point, and their lessons will probably not be supplemented by any private practice until a later stage in their training.

You will find that you and your pupil will need to go over some procedures and skills several times before he or she is reasonably proficient with a particular aspect of their driving. There will be times when the pupil will reach a 'learning plateau' where your pupil may feel that progress is not being made as well as he or she would expect. This is quite normal. For these reasons, and because driving involves such a complex mixture of tasks, learning to drive often takes longer than a lot of people appreciate.

A planned approach – which a good, professional instructor such as you will give – is an essential part of the learning process, but be prepared to persuade your pupils that they should take a certain amount of responsibility for managing their own learning by working on the theory and by practice if this is possible. You should ensure that your pupils learn in short, progressive, manageable steps initially.

You will find that 'a little and often' is a successful strategy, but it depends on the pupil's own particular circumstances. Having a lesson once every few weeks is not going to be satisfactory for them, but on the other hand cramming all the training into one marathon session is not an efficient way to learn. Two lessons each week (especially in the early stages), supplemented by the right sort of practice at the appropriate time, seems to be most suitable for most people.

Are intensive courses worthwhile?

In some circumstances, and for some people, intensive courses are satisfactory. It is the normal way with vocational driver training courses for lorries and buses, for example. Intensive courses are also used effectively for basic car driver training in the Armed Forces, the Fire and Ambulance Services and in commercial organizations where the employee can be released for a specific period of time.

This type of course does not seem to be as successful for individual learners. Although no figures are published, it seems that the test pass rate is below average.

Some people think that taking an intensive course will speed up the whole learning process. This is not necessarily the case. You will often see adverts suggesting 'start Monday – test Friday', implying that *everything* can be completed in that time. An important point to bear in mind is that the learner has to take and pass the theory test before applying for the practical part and that the application for a practical test takes several weeks in most areas. To take a 'Monday to Friday' course the pupil would need to apply for the test some time previously, and would have to take the theory test even earlier. Anyway, it's usually better to link both the theory and practical training.

As previously indicated, most experts agree that some form of spaced, regular training is more effective than a very concentrated programme. Carefully distributed practice is generally more effective than the same number of hours taken intensively. If someone really needs to take an intensive course make sure that they understand the detail of the programme before 'signing on':

- How many hours of individual practical instruction will be given?
- Is it individual instruction, or is the driving shared with someone else?
- If the test is booked for the final day, what happens if the pupil is not ready to take it?
- What happens if the pupil has to cancel the training or the test at short notice?

- What if the test is cancelled by the DSA or because of bad weather?
- What happens if the pupil fails the test?
- What if any additional training is needed during the week?

The important message is for the pupil to have an adequate amount of instruction and not to be pushed into taking a test until you both really feel that the pupil is ready.

Does private practice help?

Yes – private practice of the right type and at the appropriate time can be a great help to the learning process.

Make sure that the pupil does not start practising, though, until you feel that he or she is ready – they will need to be fairly proficient in the basics before driving a car without dual controls.

The pupil should be guided by you about what to practise. There is really not much point in them going for a long drive on a dual carriageway, for example, if you have actually indicated that they need to improve their manoeuvring skills.

Pupils will occasionally find that there is a difference of opinion about some aspects of their driving. As their instructor, you may want them to carry out a particular procedure or manoeuvre in a way that is not the same as, for example, a relative might have dealt with it. Reassure them not to worry too much about this – cars, technology and driving methods have changed quite considerably over the years. They should continue to drive in the way you have been teaching them – as a professional driver trainer you are usually better informed and more up to date with modern methods than a relative or friend. If there are any areas of real difficulty, get the pupil to discuss the differences with you. Try to avoid the pupil getting confused simply because of the way the more experienced driver does it.

Practising should take place on a wide variety of roads and in different traffic conditions – simply driving to and from work or college over the same route is not going to give pupils the variety or experience they need. Obviously this needs to be balanced with the pupil's own ability and the level of expertise that they have reached.

Does the pupil need to buy a car for practice?

Not necessarily. Having a car available for practice is obviously helpful, but it need not be one bought especially for the learner to use. If they don't have access to a car for practice it's not too much of a problem. A lot of pupils are able to complete their training and pass the test without much extra practice.

If the learner does decide to buy a car for their own use, they should find one that is going to be most suitable for their needs. They do not necessarily need to buy one simply because it's the same type as the one they are learning on. Remember that smaller, less powerful cars are going to be less expensive to insure – and this is one of the most important elements of the cost of running a car.

If the pupil has access to a family car for practice, they will probably find that it's rather different to the one that they are having lessons on. This should not be too much of a problem as long as they are reassured that, after some initial difficulty switching between the two, they will get used to the differences.

Whether the pupil is practising on their own car or one belonging to someone else, they should make sure that they are adequately covered by insurance. It should not be assumed, for example, that 'any driver' on the documents includes learners or drivers under a certain age. A careful check should be made with the insurance company or agent.

During practice sessions the pupil will need to be accompanied by a 'supervising driver'. That person must be over 21 and must have held a full licence for at least three years. It is illegal to pay someone to teach a pupil to drive unless the instructor is properly qualified.

Is special insurance needed?

Not if the pupil is having lessons with someone like yourself – a professional instructor or driving school. You will have dealt with all the arrangements for insuring the instruction car and will have made sure that both you and the pupil are covered during your lessons as well as for the examiner on the practical driving test.

During lessons the instructor is technically the person 'in charge' of the vehicle because the pupil holds only a provisional licence. If you're involved in an accident, or the pupil commits a traffic offence, you could be held to be partly responsible for your pupil's mistakes. On the driving test, however, the situation is different; this is one time when the learner is completely in charge of the car and, strictly speaking, is driving unaccompanied. As a result, the learner is totally responsible for his or her own actions.

With regard to practice on the pupil's own car, or using one belonging to someone else, that is another matter. There is then a need to have proper insurance that covers the learner driver while they are driving. The cost varies considerably, depending on a whole range of factors:

- the driver's age – the younger they are, the more costly it's likely to be;
- the make and type of vehicle being used;
- the area where the pupil lives;
- whether they have any previous driving convictions;
- how many drivers are covered by the policy;
- whether a voluntary 'excess' is in place.

The pupil should fully understand exactly what is covered (and more importantly, what is *not* covered). Check whether any excess is payable. This is the amount that would have to be paid in the event of a claim; it can be £50, £100, £250 or more, depending on the insurance company and the details of the policy.

As well as insurance, the car must be properly taxed, have a test certificate if appropriate and be completely legal and roadworthy. L plates (or D plates in Wales if preferred) must be displayed on the front and rear of the vehicle.

After passing the driving test new drivers can often benefit from reduced insurance costs by taking a course of 'Pass Plus'.

Who can help with practice?

You should give an indication of when you feel that the pupil is ready to start practising with friends or family.

While practising they will need to be accompanied by a 'supervising driver'. This person needs to be:

- over 21; and
- have held a full licence for at least three years for the type of vehicle being driven.

Make sure that pupils take your advice about how, when and what to practise. If there are any apparent discrepancies between the way you have been teaching and the way their supervising driver would drive, they should always be guided by you. ADIs are likely to be more familiar with current methods, driving procedures and test requirements than the 'amateur' instructor.

During the pupil's practice sessions they should be following the official DSA syllabus for learning and will need to refer to the Driver's Record if one is being used.

The DSA book *Helping Learners to Practise* gives a lot of valuable advice and information for anyone supervising a learner driver. For details see page 228.

Finally, the pupil should remember that they are not allowed to pay someone to help them to practise – even by paying for some petrol – unless the qualified driver is officially registered with the DSA as an ADI or a trainee licence holder.

Does the pupil need to keep special records?

Not necessarily, but it's worthwhile for them to keep a note of what needs to be practised and what you have covered during lessons.

You will be using the DSA syllabus to ensure that your training is structured and will be matching this to the individual needs of the pupil. During any practice sessions the learner should try to follow this pattern.

Ideally, you and your pupils will be using the Driver's Record. This is like a logbook of the training, including any strengths and weaknesses. Encourage the pupil to keep the Record up to date during private practice so that you are both able to accurately monitor the pupil's progress.

How much training is the pupil likely to need?

There are no hard and fast rules about how many lessons might be needed. Everyone is different and we all learn new skills at an individual rate.

One rule of thumb that has been used by the DSA and others indicates that a novice driver might need one-and-a-half hours of instruction for every year of their age. If possible, this instruction should be supplemented by good-quality practice. This, of course, is a generalization because it will depend on several factors including natural ability, the efficiency of the instructor and the quality and amount of private practice.

Pupils should take advice from you on:

- any particular topics they are not sure about;
- what books or CDs to use to supplement their training;
- when they are ready to apply for the practical test;
- how, what and when to practise;
- any training to take after passing the test; for instance motorway driving or Pass Plus.

Pupils should only take the practical test when you both feel that they are driving:

- consistently well during lessons and while practising:
- with confidence; and
- without any control or guidance from the instructor.

What is the likely cost of training?

The average cost of lessons is currently about £20 to £25 for each hour. The overall cost will probably, therefore, be in the region of £800 to £1,200 for lessons as well as the cost of a provisional licence, the theory test and one (or more!) practical tests.

What if the pupil has a disability?

You should normally be able to deal with relatively minor disabilities by offering instruction on a car with automatic transmission or by using adaptations on the steering wheel and with other small modifications.

For people with more severe disabilities – especially if they are likely to need a heavily modified car – there are several specialist organizations that can help. These include:

Queen Elizabeth's Foundation Mobility Centre
Damson Way
Fountain Drive
Carshalton
Surrey SM5 4NR
Tel: 020 8770 1151

Mobility Advice & Vehicle Information Service (MAVIS)
'O' Wing, MacAdam Avenue
Old Wokingham Road
Crowthorne
Berks RG45 6XD
Tel: 01344 661000

Edinburgh Driving Assessment Service
Astley Ainslie Hospital
133 Grange Loan
EDINBURGH EH9 2HL
Tel: 0131 537 9192

and many more local organizations and services.

There are so many different types of modification available that most people with disabilities can be catered for.

PASS PLUS

As soon as your pupil has passed their test you should encourage them to take Pass Plus. This should be regarded as an essential part of their driver training programme. It is an opportunity for them to have training in some of the subjects that are not always available to them in preparation for the L test.

What is it?

Pass Plus was set up by the DSA to encourage young drivers to take more training immediately after passing their test. The scheme gives the new driver more experience in a wider range of situations and conditions than is required for the driving test. For example, learner drivers are not allowed to drive on motorways, so these are included as part of the Pass Plus syllabus.

Who runs it?

The scheme is operated and managed by the Driving Standards Agency with support from the driving instruction industry and many motor insurance companies. Individual instructors are specially registered by the DSA to carry out the required instruction by following a specific programme of training for the pupil.

What benefits are there?

There are educational and training benefits by experiencing different road and traffic conditions such as motorways and faster moving, multi-lane traffic conditions.

The main financial benefit is that the new driver can obtain very substantial discounts on motor insurance by taking Pass Plus within a limited time after passing the test.

Full details of participating insurance companies are given at the end of this section.

What is it likely to cost?

The full programme of training usually costs a little more than the cost of six driving lessons, but this seems to vary from one instructor to another and in different parts of the country. The reason for the extra cost and the variation in prices is due to the extra mileage (in particular for the motorway driving element) involved in the Pass Plus programme compared with L driver lessons.

Is it a test?

No. It's a structured programme of training tailored to the pupil's specific needs. The course consists of six modules, covering:

- *In town* – learn how to cope with town driving.
- *In all weather* – learn about the problems of winter driving, including fog, ice and snow.
- *Out of town* – dealing with country roads, wildlife and farm vehicles.
- *At night* – reading the road in the dark and dusk.
- *On dual carriageways* – making progress, separation distances, lane discipline.

- *Motorways* – driving skills, observations, anticipation, planning and concentration.

The pupil has to achieve a reasonable standard in each module. After satisfactorily completing the course the instructor notifies DSA who issue a certificate. This enables the driver to obtain the discount from their preferred insurance company.

More details about Pass Plus are available at www.passplus.org.uk or by telephone on 0115 936 6504.

Do I need to register separately as a Pass Plus instructor?

Yes – to conduct Pass Plus courses instructors do not necessarily have to have any special training or take a separate exam, but they have to be specially registered with the DSA.

When should Pass Plus be taken?

Pupils should take Pass Plus as soon as possible after passing the driving test. This is when they will get the most benefit from the training.

In any event, to obtain the insurance discount benefit, the pupil will normally need to take the course within one year of passing the practical driving test.

Pass Plus insurance companies

Insurer	Telephone	website
AA insurance	0800 197 6173	theaa.com
Adrian Flux Ins Services	08700 764841	adrianflux.co.uk
Churchill Insurance	0800 200 331	churchill.co.uk
C I S	08457 464646	cis.co.uk
Direct Line	020 8686 3313	directline.com
Endsleigh	0800 783 6414	endsleigh.co.uk
Norwich Union	0800 096 4715	norwichunion.com
Privilege	0845 246 0311	privilege.com
Provident	01422 331 166	providentinsurance.co.uk
RAC direct insurance	0800 404 6796	rac.co.uk
Royal & Sun Alliance	0800 072 4186	morethan.com
Swinton	0800 0565 631	swinton.co.uk
Tesco Motor Insurers	0845 300 4400	tescofinance.com
Quinn Dir Ins	0845 850 0845	quinn-direct.co.uk
Young marmalade	0845 644 2026	youngmarmalade.co.uk
Zurich	0800 445 588	eaglestar.co.uk

WHAT NEXT – AFTER THE TEST

How does the pupil obtain a full licence?

At the end of the practical test the examiner will offer to have a full licence issued automatically. The examiner issues a pass certificate and the full licence will be sent by DVLA within about three weeks. There is no fee for this service, but it can only be done in this way if the photo-card licence was issued after 1 March 2004.

If the provisional licence was issued earlier, or the pupil prefers to make an individual application, the pass certificate and licence must be sent to DVLA as soon as possible. Make sure to make a note of the details of any documents (or keep a photocopy). In either case, the driver is allowed to drive unaccompanied while DVLA are dealing with the issue of a full licence.

The application should be sent to: DVLA, Swansea SA99 1AB.

What does a full licence cover?

A full Category B car licence allows the holder to drive passenger vehicles with up to eight passenger seats and goods vehicles up to 3,500 kg.

To drive larger vehicles it is necessary to take another test – for example, a B+E test for towing trailers or C1 for medium-sized goods vehicles.

The minimum age for driving a large goods vehicle (category C – over 7.5 tonnes) is 21.

For full details of licence categories and minimum driving ages, see the DVLA website at www.dvla.gov.uk.

What is the cost of a licence?

There is no fee for exchanging a provisional licence for the first full licence.

An exchange licence – for adding a test pass or removing an expired endorsement is £17.50. Renewing a licence after disqualification is £65.

What vehicles are the new driver not allowed to drive?

With a category B car licence the driver is not allowed to drive a vehicle with more than eight passenger seats or a goods vehicle over 3,500 kg gross weight.

What about towing a trailer?

The maximum weight of any trailer for use with a category B licence is 750 kg.

What about driving larger vehicles?

To drive a goods vehicle over 3,500 kg gross weight or a passenger vehicle with more than eight seats the minimum age is 18. The driver needs to obtain the appropriate provisional licence entitlement, take another theory test (for goods vehicles or for passenger vehicles) and finally another practical test on the appropriate type of vehicle.

The licence entitlement will then be for passenger vehicles up to 17 seats or goods vehicles up to 7.5 tonnes. For driving any vehicles larger than this the minimum age is 21.

What advanced driving courses are available?

The DSA recommend that all new drivers should take the Pass Plus course soon after passing their L test.

Apart from taking Pass Plus there are several advanced driving qualifications that could be considered.

The Institute of Advanced Motorists is a voluntary organization that offers an advanced driving test for drivers who have a reasonable amount of experience. Details are available at www.iam.org.uk or on 0845 126 8600.

An alternative is the RoSPA Advanced Driving Test. This has a unique system of grading successful candidates as 'gold', 'silver' or 'bronze'. More information can be obtained at www.rospa.co.uk or on 0121 248 2000.

What is the situation with penalty points?

Any driver who accumulates 12 or more penalty points within a three-year period will automatically be disqualified under the 'totting' procedure for a minimum of six months. The disqualification is mandatory unless there are exceptional personal circumstances.

What is 'The New Driver Act (1995)'?

The Act affects any newly qualified driver who accumulates six or more penalty points within two years of passing their test. If this happens the licence is automatically revoked by DVLA and the driver would have to revert to a provisional licence. This means starting again by retaking the theory and practical tests.

What about driving abroad?

A lot of other countries have a minimum driving age that is higher than ours in the UK.

In European Union countries you can drive on a UK licence, but many other countries will require an International Driving Permit. In this case you would normally need to be over 18.

More information on driving abroad (and on visitors to the UK) is in *The Driving Instructor's Handbook*.

For full details about driving abroad and IDPs, contact the AA or RAC. Their details are given on page 222.

SPEED LIMITS

What are the speed limits on different types of road?

A speed limit of 30 mph normally applies where there is regular street lighting. If there is a higher limit on this type of road there will be repeater signs showing the maximum speed. If there are no street lights but a speed limit exists there will be repeater signs showing the limit.

Unless otherwise indicated the national speed limit on single carriageways is 60 mph. On dual carriageways and motorways the limit is 70 mph. These limits apply to cars and car-derived vans up to 2 tonnes maximum laden weight.

Are they any different for other vehicles?

Yes. If you tow a trailer behind your car the speed limit on single carriageway roads is 50 mph and 60 mph on dual carriageways and motorways. You are not allowed to use the third lane of a three-lane motorway with this combination because of the lower speed

When driving a medium-sized goods vehicle (over 2 tonnes maximum weight and up to 7.5 tonnes) the maximum speed is:

- single carriageway – 50 mph;
- dual carriageway – 60 mph;
- motorway – 70 mph.

Large goods vehicles (over 7.5 tonnes) have lower speed limits.

Why are speed limits important?

Speed limits are imposed on residential and urban areas to make the roads safer for all road users, particularly pedestrians. Because stopping distances are much greater at higher speeds, driving at a speed that is too fast for the conditions is potentially dangerous.

Remember to reduce your speed where there are potential hazards and in poor weather conditions and at night.

Speed limits:

Type of vehicle	Single carriageway	Dual carriageway	Motorway
Car & motorcycle (including car-derived van)	60	70	70
Car with trailer or caravan	50	60	60
Goods vehicle up to 7.5 tonnes	50	60	70
Goods vehicle and trailer	50	60	60
Large goods vehicle (over 7.5 tonnes)	40	50	60
Bus/coach (up to 12 metres)	50	60	70
Bus/coach (over 12 metres)	50	60	60

STOPPING DISTANCES

What do I need to know?

'Stopping distance' is measured from when you first realized that you have to brake to the point where your vehicle eventually stops. This overall distance depends on a number of factors including the speed you're travelling, the condition of your vehicle, the weather and road conditions, and your reaction time in response to developing conditions.

The stopping distance is the total of thinking distance and braking distance.

Thinking distance varies from one person to another, but is generally about two-thirds of a second. In this time, at 30 mph, you'll travel about nine metres. The distance increases proportionally with speed, so at 60 mph the distance will be about 18 metres. If you're travelling at 70 mph on a motorway you will cover about 21 metres (about five to six car lengths) before you even start braking. If you are tired, or are not fully concentrating, your reaction time will be slower and the distance covered will be greater.

Braking distance depends on the speed you're travelling at. At 20 mph the braking distance is about 6 metres, but this increases to 24 metres at 40 mph. In other words, by doubling your speed the braking distance is four times greater. At 70 mph the braking distance for a car in normal driving conditions will be about 75 metres. On wet or slippery roads these distances will be much longer.

Stopping distances:

Speed (mph)	Thinking distance (metres)	Braking distance (metres)	Overall stopping distance (metres)
20	6	6	12
30	9	14	23
40	12	24	36
50	15	38	53
60	18	55	73
70	21	75	96

From the chart you can see that:

- thinking distance increases proportionally with the speed;
- braking distance increases at a much greater rate.

This means that if you double your speed from 30 mph to 60 mph the braking distance is nearly four times as much.

What is 'separation distance'?

This is the distance you should keep between yourself and the vehicle in front. Ideally, this distance should be the same as the overall stopping distance – which is about 96 metres when travelling at 70 mph. In busy traffic conditions this is not always practicable, but the gap should always be at *least* the thinking distance.

A lot of drivers use the 'two second' rule to judge the appropriate gap. This involves checking when the vehicle in front passes a particular reference point and then counting two seconds before you pass that same point.

In poor weather conditions this distance should be increased to four seconds.

If someone behind is travelling much too close, you should leave more of a gap between you and the vehicle in front. This is to ensure that the total gap between the three vehicles is sufficient.

Can I stop quicker if my car is fitted with ABS?

Anti-lock braking systems are designed to make sure that maximum braking is applied, but that the wheels do not lose their grip in normal conditions. They allow you to steer at the same time as braking firmly, so you are much safer in controlling the car in an emergency situation. They do not necessarily stop the car any quicker.

Are skidpan lessons beneficial?

Skidpans are very good for simulating at relatively low speeds the situations that you might be faced with at higher speeds on the road. You can practise the different types of skid in a controlled environment without any other traffic involved. They can also be great fun!

On a skidpan you learn what makes the car skid, and therefore how *not* to skid. When you're driving on the road – with other traffic about – you should be able to avoid getting into situations where you might skid.

MOTORWAYS

Is motorway driving any different?

Yes. Motorways are designed to allow traffic to move much more freely than on other roads. There are no junctions, crossroads, roundabouts, pedestrians or cyclists and slower moving vehicles such as tractors and mopeds are not allowed to use them. Learner drivers are also prohibited.

Because the traffic is moving more quickly – and in several lanes – you need to be aware of the traffic conditions around you at all times. Traffic will be joining the motorway at fairly high speed from slip roads on the left and following vehicles will be closing on you much more rapidly than on normal roads.

During their driving lessons pupils will not have had the opportunity to drive on motorways. This is one of the benefits of taking a Pass Plus course soon after passing the driving test.

Pupils who have not been able to take advantage of Pass Plus should be encouraged to arrange a motorway lesson. They will find this beneficial as it will introduce them to the requirements of motorway driving – lane discipline, entering and leaving, lane closures, motorway signs – before being left to deal with these new situations on their own.

Most ADIs find that they can offer instruction in motorway driving. The length of a lesson will depend on a number of factors including how far away from a suitable motorway you are and how you normally programme this type of training alongside your other work.

Can I take my pupils on motorways before they pass the driving test?

No. Learner drivers are restricted to driving on non-motorway roads. During their lessons you can use multi-lane dual carriageways with faster-moving traffic, but this is not quite the same as driving on motorways.

After passing the test pupils are recommended to take Pass Plus as a main part of the syllabus covers motorway driving.

DRINK/DRIVING

What are the important factors?

Driving with alcohol in the blood can be potentially dangerous. Without necessarily realizing it, your ability to drive safely will be reduced. Alcohol has the effect of slowing down your reactions and can affect your judgement of speed and distance. At the same time it tends to give a false sense of confidence.

What are the legal limits?

You will be committing a serious offence if you drive with a breath/alcohol level of more than 35 microgrammes per 100 millilitre. This is the equivalent of 80 mgs to 100 ml in terms of blood/alcohol.

Alcohol takes some time to leave the body. Some alcohol may be left in the bloodstream a considerable time after drinking, such as the morning after consuming alcohol in the evening.

What are the penalties?

For a drink/drive offence a court *must* disqualify you from driving for a minimum of one year. If there was a high reading, or for a repeated offence, the disqualification would be much longer. For a second offence within a ten-year period the court must disqualify for a minimum of three years.

As well as the disqualification there will be a heavy financial penalty and most people in this situation find that insuring their car at the end of the disqualification period may be difficult. At best the disqualified driver can expect to pay much more and at worst the insurance company may refuse to renew the insurance cover.

SEAT BELTS AND CHILD RESTRAINTS

What is the law on seat belts?

Seat belts have been fitted in all new cars since 1987. It is a legal requirement for the driver and passengers to use the seat belt.

The driver of the vehicle and adult passengers are individually responsible for wearing their own seat belt.

In the case of children under the age of 14, it is the driver's responsibility to make sure that the seat belt or child restraint is used.

Why is it important to use them?

If you are involved in an accident, statistics show that you are much safer if you are wearing a seat belt.

In addition, the wearing of a seat belt can be a factor in the assessment of compensation following an accident. Courts have often reduced the amount of compensation for someone not wearing a belt.

Are there any exemptions?

Yes, there are several exemptions from the requirement to wear a seat belt.

These exemptions include:

- drivers or passengers with a medical exemption certificate;
- drivers of delivery vehicles covering short distances and making multiple stops;
- when carrying out a manoeuvre that includes reversing;
- supervising a learner driver carrying out a reverse manoeuvre;
- driving test examiners (but not instructors).

There are several other exemptions covering disabled drivers, taxi drivers, and police and emergency service drivers.

What is the situation with child restraints?

Children under the age of 12 are allowed to travel in the front seat of a car if they use an appropriate child seat or cushion.

A child under the age of 12 has to be at least 4' 5" (1.5m) in height before he or she is allowed to travel without a child seat or a booster cushion.

It is legal for children to travel in the back of a car without car seats or a cushion, but only if the car is not fitted with seat belts. It is not recommended, though, because it is regarded as potentially unsafe.

Child's age	Front seat	Rear seat
Under the age of 3	Appropriate child restraint must be used	Appropriate child restraint must be used
3 to 11 and under 4' 5"	Appropriate child restraint must be used	Appropriate child restraint must be used if available
Child aged 12 to 13 or child 4' 5" or more in height	Adult seat belt must be used if available.	Adult seat belt must be used if available.

How would I choose the right child seat?

It's always the weight of the child and not the age that dictates the choice of seat. Check at regular intervals whether you need to change the seat.

All seats are divided into numbered groups (0 to 3) for different weights of child.

Would it be more cost effective to buy second hand?

All responsible bodies agree and recommend that you should not buy (or sell) used child seats as you can never be sure of the history of the seat. Many child seats sold through local advertising and at car boot sales have been found to be potentially dangerous.

ACCIDENTS

What do I need to do at the scene?

If you're involved in an accident you must stop – even if you think that it's only minor.

If you are one of the first at the scene of an accident you will need to warn other traffic of the obstruction by switching on hazard warning lights and by displaying an advance warning. You might need to arrange other means of controlling approaching traffic.

Call the emergency services, making sure that you give accurate details of the location. On a motorway, refer to the emergency telephone reference number as well as the nearest junction number.

Move any uninjured people away from the vehicles. On a motorway this means well away from the road, the hard shoulder and the central reservation.

Do I need to report to the police?

The legal definition of an 'accident' is one that causes injury to another person or animal, or one that causes damage to another person's vehicle or property.

If you are involved in an accident you must give your name, address and vehicle details. If there is personal injury, your insurance details must be given to anyone who has reasonable cause to see them. You must also give information about the ownership of the vehicle. If it is not possible to exchange these details at the time, the accident must be reported to the police as soon as possible, and in any case within 24 hours.

If the accident involves damage to another person's property or injury to an animal you must exchange details with the owner. If this is not done you must report the accident to the police.

ECO-DRIVING

What is eco-driving?

We can all reduce exhaust emissions by driving in a way that's environmentally friendly. Eco-friendly driving can make a significant impact on the global use of conventional carbon-based fuels and make a positive contribution to the reduction of carbon emissions. This process starts with an awareness of the availability of vehicles with alternative fuels such as electric and 'dual-fuel' power.

How should I adjust my driving?

To make an improvement in your fuel-efficient driving there are several areas to be considered, including:

Use the *accelerator* in a steady, smooth and progressive way, avoiding any unnecessary speed peaks. A smooth driving style can save up to 10 per cent of the fuel used.

Your use of the *footbrake* should be smooth and positive, with a certain amount of tapering on and off. Avoid any harsh use of the brake by easing off the accelerator a little earlier.

Gear changes should be made effectively, with block changes up and down where appropriate. Move into the higher gears reasonably quickly. Cars with manual gears are generally more fuel-efficient than those with automatic gears.

Hazard awareness and forward-planning techniques should be used effectively to minimize any unnecessary or harsh changes of speed or direction.

Vehicle sympathy. Engine speeds should be kept relatively low whenever possible. In general, keeping the engine speed to about 3,000 rpm can save a considerable amount of fuel. All the controls should be used smoothly to avoid any unnecessary sharp fluctuations in speed.

Manoeuvring. Reversing into a parking space and then driving out forwards is more fuel-efficient than reversing out when the engine is cold.

Speed. Keep to all legal speed limits and plan well ahead for any changes. Some experts suggest that by reducing your top speed from 80 mph to 70 mph you can save a considerable amount of fuel.

Air conditioning. Avoid using the air con or climate control unless it is necessary, as this can be detrimental to fuel consumption. Avoid driving at speed with the windows or sunroof open as this can create drag and an increase in the amount of fuel used.

Remember – this is not just about saving fuel in your own vehicle, it's more to do with releasing less pollutants into the atmosphere and conserving fuel globally.

Why is good maintenance important?

Keeping the engine running efficiently and having tyres inflated correctly can help with fuel efficiency and cost savings.

Can I save money?

Yes, we can all use less fuel by using environmentally friendly driving techniques. It is estimated that you can save up to 30 per cent of fuel costs by applying effective techniques such as avoiding harsh braking and excessive acceleration.

Individually, the savings may not seem much, but collectively they can make substantial reductions, not only in your own costs, but also on the global use of carbon fuels.

9

Business opportunities

This chapter includes details of the various business opportunities available to supplement learner driver training.

Although most driving instructors concentrate solely on teaching learner drivers, there are many other opportunities for increasing your scope of work. As well as adding variety alongside your regular work in driver training, these other activities will offer the opportunity for additional revenue and income streams to your business.

Some of the areas you might consider (and which are covered in this chapter) include:

- pre-driver training;
- intensive courses
- Pass Plus;
- learning materials;
- minibus driver training;
- trailer and caravan towing;
- company and fleet driver training;
- taxi driver assessment;
- LGV driver training.

Other possible business opportunities (which are covered in more detail in *The Driving Instructor's Handbook*, Kogan Page, 2009) are:

- training for people who have a disability;
- defensive and advanced driver training;
- assessments for older drivers;
- driver training schemes for local authorities;
- corrective and driver-rehabilitation courses.

Which of these you decide to offer will depend on your individual interests, experience, qualifications or expertise.

PRE-DRIVER TRAINING

If you have access to any off-road facility such as a large private car park, school grounds or a disused airfield, you may be able to offer pre-driver training for under-17s. Training would normally be more cost-effective for groups of pupils rather than one-to-one instruction, so target your local youth groups and schools – through the head teacher or direct with the education authority. If you have a local road safety group it would be worthwhile liaising with them for course content and for marketing or promotion purposes. It is often beneficial to work with one or more other instructors in your area and to organize the course as part theory and part practical. This has the added benefit of working on attitudes in addition to practical vehicle control skills at an early age. Even if you only have a relatively small training area available, it is still possible to organize the course programme with an emphasis on lower-speed manoeuvring.

INTENSIVE L DRIVER COURSE

Offering intensive courses can be a useful way of generating extra business for your school – particularly if you are based in an area that people would like to visit.

Before considering this particular business opportunity, you need to be aware of a few important points:

- If you offer a one-week intensive course with the practical driving test on the final day, the pupil must have already passed the theory test.
- The customer should be made aware that they might not be ready to take the test – in which case, the fee would be lost.
- Full payment should be taken in advance as you will not want to risk having an empty diary for the whole week.
- Intensive courses are, by their nature, hard work for both the pupil and the instructor. Not everyone responds to them effectively – many pupils would be better off with a less concentrated programme of training consisting of two or three hours of instruction each day over a longer period.
- Intensive or concentrated courses involve having the same customer with you for an extended period – possibly all day, every day for a week or more. You will need to deal with this situation – even with a client who you do not particularly like, or who may have personal hygiene problems.

PASS PLUS

This subject is dealt with from the pupil's perspective in Chapter 8 – *L Driver Training*.

If you are going to offer Pass Plus as an extra course of post-test training make sure that you educate your pupils (and their parents) at an early stage. There is little point in introducing the subject once the pupil has passed the driving test. Make it clear from the start of the training that Pass Plus is regarded as an important and integral part of the whole process of learning to drive.

Pass Plus was originally set up by the Driving Standards Agency in an effort to encourage new drivers to take further training rather than regarding the driving test as the end of the learning process. The intention was (and still is) for the pupil to be trained in a wider range of road and traffic conditions than those that are tested in the ordinary driving test. The course builds on the pupil's existing skills and knowledge and so should be tailored to individual requirements. Although there is no exam at the end of the course, the pupil is assessed by the instructor in each of the modules and must reach an acceptable standard.

Pupils can be encouraged to take the extra training by making sure that they realize the benefit of the extra training and the financial benefit of substantial discounts that many insurance companies offer.

Anyone who holds a full UK licence can take part, but it is usual for pupils to take the course shortly after passing the driving test. By doing this, the new driver can qualify for the special insurance rates.

Your fees for Pass Plus should be more than your normal hourly rate. This is because you will be using more fuel; travelling longer distances; and will have an element of office work and DSA fees to cover. As well as this, there is the probability that the night driving element of the course will involve out-of-hours work.

Pass Plus syllabus

Town driving:

- observations, judgement and awareness;
- vulnerable road users;
- keeping space around you.

All-weather driving:

- appropriate speed;
- safe stopping distances;
- rain, sleet, snow, ice;

- mist and fog;
- skids and prevention;
- bright sunlight.

Driving out of town:

- observations;
- making progress;
- bends, hills, uneven surfaces, dead ground;
- safe distances;
- pedestrians, horse riders, animals;
- farm entrances, slow-moving vehicles.

Night driving:

- correct use of headlights;
- adjusting to dark conditions;
- judgement of speed and distance;
- use and care of lights;
- dealing with dazzle;
- parking.

Dual carriageways:

- effective observations;
- use of mirrors, blind areas;
- judgement and planning;
- safe separation distances;
- joining and leaving;
- lane discipline, overtaking;
- use of speed.

Motorways:

- advance journey planning;
- joining and leaving;
- using slip roads safely and effectively;
- safe speeds;
- all-round observations;
- signs, signals and markings;
- overtaking, lane discipline;
- courtesy, fatigue;
- breakdowns;
- lights and hazard warning lights;
- crosswinds.

The course takes a minimum of six hours, but more sessions might be needed for some pupils to attain a satisfactory standard.

The Pass Plus course can be taken at any time up to 12 months after passing the practical L test and any insurance discount can be deferred for a further two years if the new driver is driving on another person's insurance.

Although the number of drivers taking Pass Plus is gradually increasing, it is still a market where only a minority of instructors take advantage of the potential for extra business.

Instructors who are actively involved in the scheme emphasize the need to:

- mention Pass Plus and the benefits when pupils first enquire about lessons;
- involve parents at an early stage, getting them to understand the added reassurance that Pass Plus offers;
- remind pupils about the scheme before and after they take the L test;

- inform pupils and parents of the statistics on newly qualified drivers being involved in a disproportionate number of accidents.

To register as a Pass Plus instructor, you need to apply to the DSA for a starter pack.

LEARNING MATERIALS

The multiple choice theory test and hazard perception test are both computer-based and most pupils will have access to a computer, whether at home, work, school or college. It is therefore beneficial for you to offer the appropriate materials for learning.

Various CDs and DVDs are available for the hazard perception test and for the multiple-choice theory test. Have some of each of these available for your pupils to practise on. Whether you lend, sell or hire them to pupils will depend on your business plan. Do you want to make additional income, or is it a promotional tool?

MINIBUSES

Anyone who held a full driving licence before 1 January 1997 has entitlement to drive minibuses with up to 16 passenger seats if the vehicle is not used for hire or reward. Drivers who have passed their L test since January 1997 are allowed to drive vehicles with up to eight passenger seats. Many minibuses belonging to schools, youth groups and community groups have vehicles with more seats and these can all be potential customers. Instruction can usually be carried out in the customer's own vehicle, but be particularly careful of any insurance issues.

Remember, you must have held a licence for that type of vehicle for at least three years.

CAR AND CARAVAN OR TRAILER

Drivers who passed the car-driving test before 1 January 1997 are allowed to drive a vehicle and trailer combination up to 8.25 tonnes maximum authorized mass (MAM).

MAM is usually taken to mean the maximum permissible weight, which is also known as gross vehicle weight.

For licences issued after 1 January 1997, the driver is restricted in the type of trailer or combination used:

- A car may be coupled with a trailer of up to 750 kg MAM as long as the combined weight is not more than 4.25 kg

or

- The trailer may be over 750 kg, provided that the MAM of the trailer does not exceed the unladen weight of the towing vehicle and the combined weight does not exceed 3.5 tonnes MAM.

The effect of these regulations is that *most* caravans and small trailers towed by cars on a category B licence should be within the threshold, but, if not, a separate licence for category B + E must be obtained. This entails higher medical standards and a separate driving test with the car and trailer must be taken.

FLEET DRIVER TRAINING

For anyone wanting to expand his or her business opportunities, fleet training is a particularly interesting and rewarding area of driver training.

The Fleet Driver Training Register is operated on similar lines to the ADI Register, but with particular emphasis on coaching and assessment.

Once you have qualified as an ADI and have had experience in providing training to car and van drivers you can apply to join the Register of Fleet Driver Trainers. This is a voluntary scheme run by the DSA. Its aims are to improve road safety by monitoring the standards and training of fleet driver training providers.

To qualify for the Register you must be currently registered with the DSA as an ADI.

There are two separate ways of qualifying: by taking the qualifying exams direct with the DSA or by completing an approved training course with a DSA-accredited provider. If you take the option of attending a training course you must make sure the provider is accredited by the DSA. A full list of course providers is on the DSA website (www.dsa.gov.uk and follow the link to 'fleet register').

The exams are similar to the ADI exams; a theory test, practical driving test and practical coaching/assessment test.

A maximum of three attempts is allowed for each part of the exam and all three parts must be passed within 12 months.

Full details of the Fleet Training Register, including the question bank, are available from the DSA. Send a cheque or postal order for £6.99 to: Fleet Driver Training Register, Driving Standards Agency, The Axis Building, 112 Upper Parliament Street, Nottingham, NG1 6LP.

As well as formal fleet training, there is also the possibility of offering training individually to local companies, education departments, health authorities as in-service, ongoing training or as pre-employment assessments.

TAXI DRIVER ASSESSMENTS

The DSA offer a special driving assessment for taxi drivers consisting of a practical drive lasting about 35 to 40 minutes. Some of the skills that are assessed are specific to taxi driving such as making a

U-turn and not stopping anywhere that would be dangerous for the passenger.

The driver is tested on his or her knowledge of the Highway Code and is also asked to identify several road signs and markings.

During the assessment, the driver is checked on:

- awareness and anticipation;
- effective planning of the prevailing road and traffic conditions;
- correct use of speed;
- emergency stop;
- a manoeuvre involving reversing;
- passenger comfort and safety.

If the taxi is suitably fitted there will be an assessment of wheelchair usage.

The driver needs to complete the assessment with no more than nine minor faults and with no serious or dangerous faults.

Many local authorities are now using this special assessment and you may well find that there is scope in your area for carrying out pre-assessment training and appraisals.

LGV TRAINING

An ordinary driving licence nowadays covers the driver for vehicles up to three tonnes gross weight. For any vehicle over that weight, a special category of licence and a separate test is required.

Vehicles over three tonnes fall into different categories of licence:

- C1 – medium-sized goods vehicle;
- C1 + E – medium-sized vehicle with trailer;
- C – rigid large goods vehicle;
- C + E – articulated large goods vehicle or rigid LGV with trailer.

The only statutory requirement for instructing on lorries is to have held a licence for that category of vehicle for at least three years.

A 'voluntary register of LGV instructors' is operated by the DSA, but it is purely voluntary at the present time.

Compulsory training and retraining of LGV drivers was introduced in 2009 as part of the Driver Certificate of Competence regulations and this will, almost certainly, have an impact on the demand for driver training for this category of driver – both for initial instruction in preparation for the driving test and for refresher training for full licence holders.

The LGV Voluntary Register

The Register has been running for over 10 years. Its aim is to raise the standard of training for lorry drivers. Testing and monitoring of the scheme is carried out by specialist DSA examiners who have particular LGV experience.

You can apply for inclusion on the Register if you hold a full category C1 (medium-sized goods vehicle), category C1+ E (medium-sized goods vehicle with trailer), category C (rigid goods vehicle) or a full category C + E (articulated large goods vehicle or large goods vehicle with trailer) licence.

To qualify for the Register you must hold a full, unrestricted licence for the category of vehicle in which you intend to instruct. You must not have been disqualified from driving at any time in the previous four years, must have held the appropriate licence for at least three years and must be over 21.

As with the ADI exam, there are three parts to the qualifying exams:

- theory test and hazard perception test;
- practical test of your own driving ability;
- practical test of instructional ability.

You are allowed a maximum of three attempts at each part of the exam and you must pass all three parts within one year.

To apply to join the Register, a starter pack (currently costing £6.99) is available from the LGV Register Section, DSA, The Axis Building, 112 Upper Parliament Street, Nottingham, NG1 6LP.

The starter pack includes the application forms, notes for guidance and the theory test question bank.

10

Continuing professional development

After qualifying as an ADI you should continue to work at improving and updating your skills both as an instructor and as a business owner. This chapter gives a few ideas on how to achieve those objectives.

Continuing professional development (CPD) is generally regarded as:

> A conscious updating of professional knowledge and an improvement of professional competence throughout a person's working life.

It also involves:

- an ongoing commitment to being professional;
- keeping up to date with information and best practices;
- constantly seeking to improve.

CPD is driven by the individual person's own learning and development needs.

A lot of work is currently being undertaken to review the needs of instructors in the area of CPD, including various projects commissioned by the DSA and the Department for Transport (DfT). The results of these projects should be known and implemented soon, but there are already a few indicators that have emerged. One of the main points is that there is currently no real incentive for ADIs to develop their skills and, in fact, only a very small percentage undertake any form of qualification or training other than the basic DSA qualification. The general trend in most other industries and professions is for CPD to be much more widely undertaken (and is an expectation for most people). For example, in the road transport industry there is a European directive that will require all lorry drivers to take a minimum amount of refresher training every few years. This training will include an element of business knowledge and customer care skills. There is clearly a need for more training and development for instructors but, as always, it is uncertain how any CPD courses or initiatives will be funded, because it is extremely unlikely that the majority of instructors will take training or extra qualifications unless they are obliged to or are motivated in some way. Nevertheless it can be shown that CPD is now even more important in a world that is very competitive.

Any properly prepared programme of CPD for driving instruction should include an element of business and customer care skills as well as the personal and instructional skills that are covered in more detail in *Practical Teaching Skills for Driving Instructors*. These subjects include:

- personal skills:
- assertive skills;
- affective skills;
- problem-solving skills;
- decision-making skills;
- feedback;
- own driving skills;
- instructor training;
- role-play skills.

As an ongoing process, the DSA is actively encouraging all driver trainers to participate in CPD. Their recommendations include keeping records. Sample forms for recording details of CPD are available from the DSA. These records include:

- the type of activity;
- total hours;
- competence type;
- application of what was learned;
- impact on career or business.

Join a local and/or national association to keep informed on CPD developments. You will find contact details of the main instructor organizations on page 218 and a summary of activities later in the next section of this chapter.

Being involved with an ongoing programme of CPD can be a useful marketing and selling point for your business. For example, the DSA has introduced a 'find your nearest instructor' facility on their website. Through this database, which is part of the DSA's integrated register of driver trainers, it is possible for prospective pupils to access details of their local ADIs and to see at a glance whether someone has signed up for CPD. Being involved with CPD shows the potential pupil that you are being professional and are keeping up to date.

CPD can include the development of communication skills, eco-friendly driving, special needs training and business development. You do not necessarily have to attend a formal training course; your involvement can be through informal training or by way of home study.

It is up to you as an individual to decide what type of CPD is most appropriate to your needs and the way you want to undertake it. However, bear in mind that CPD is an ongoing activity and that the DSA recommend that you should have a minimum of seven hours of CPD training each year.

Apart from formal training courses, CPD can be undertaken in a variety of different ways, including:

- attendance at local or national meetings and seminars;
- spending time developing business skills;
- updating teaching, coaching or driving skills;
- attending formal training courses;
- networking with other instructors.

To move the programme forward, the DSA is working closely with ADI representative groups, sector skills councils and various other bodies to research and develop more proposals for a structured CPD scheme that will eventually become compulsory.

ADI ASSOCIATIONS

Several main organizations are open to individual membership, including:

- The Approved Driving Instructors National Joint Council (ADI NJC);
- Driving Instructors Association (DIA);
- The Motor Schools Association of GB (MSA).

ADI NJC

The ADI NJC is a non-profit organization with no commercial interests and no salaried staff.

Membership consists of local instructor associations, each of which has representation, with each member organization having a vote at meetings.

Individual ADIs can also take part by joining the Driving Instructors' Group, which is a section of the ADI NJC. The group has a separate secretary who looks after DIA members and who represents them at meetings.

Contact details:

Approved Driving Instructors National Joint Council (NJC)
General Secretary
16 Grosvenor Close
LICHFIELD
Staffordshire WS14 9SR
Tel: 01543 256578.
www.adinjc.com.

DIA

The Driving Instructors Association was formed in 1978 and is now regarded as the largest trade association for professional driver trainers in the UK. Membership is open to all ADIs and anyone training for the ADI qualification. Although the DIA is a proprietary association, it is guided by a General Purposes Committee that is elected from the membership. Staff members carry out the main work of the organization.

Each individual member receives regular copies of *Driving* magazine and *Driving Instructor*. Services provided include training courses and conferences as well as special rates on car, breakdown and health insurance.

Contact details:

Driving Instructors Association (DIA)
Safety House
Beddington Farm Road
CROYDON
Surrey CR0 4XY
Tel: 0208 665 5151.
www.driving.org.

MSA

The Motor Schools Association was formed in 1935, about the time the driving test was introduced.

Full membership is available only to fully qualified ADIs, but trainee instructors may join as temporary members. The Association's main aims are:

- to represent members at all levels of government;
- to provide services that will be of benefit to members;
- to set standards of professional and ethical behaviour for professional driver trainers.

Every member receives a copy of the monthly publication *MSA Newslink* and a copy of the Association's handbook.

The MSA offers a wide range of services, including professional indemnity insurance, vehicle equipment and special discounts on trainer-related products and services.

Contact details:

Motor Schools Association of GB (MSA)
101 Wellington Road North
STOCKPORT
Cheshire SK4 2LP
Tel: 0161 429 9669.
www.msagb.co.uk.

Local associations

As well as joining one (or more) of the national associations, you should consider getting involved with your local association. This is a good way of keeping up to date with what is happening in your local area and of networking with other instructors, both of which can be part of any programme of CPD.

For details of local associations, check in your test centre or contact one of the main national associations who will be able to provide details.

Local associations in Scotland can be located by contacting DISC – the Driving Instructors Scottish Council at 4 Burnside Road, Uphall Broxburn, West Lothian EH52 5DE. Telephone: 01506 855455; Web: www.d-i-s-c.org.uk.

ADVANCED DRIVING TESTS

To make sure that your own driving skills are up to date, consider taking one (or more!) of the advanced driving tests that are widely available.

Special Cardington driving test

The Cardington test is specially designed and operated by the Driving Standards Agency for ADIs who – as part of their ongoing CPD – want to demonstrate that they have a high standard of driving competency.

The test is conducted in your own car and is carried out by a specially trained staff member at the DSA training centre at Cardington, Bedfordshire. It involves about 90 minutes of practical driving on all types of road, including motorways, and in a variety of traffic conditions.

To pass the test, you have to show a positive, courteous attitude and the ability to control the position and speed of the vehicle safely, systematically and smoothly. In particular, you are assessed on your:

- expert handling of the controls;
- use of correct road position;
- anticipation of the actions of other road users and taking appropriate action;

- sound judgement of distance, speed and timing;
- consideration for the convenience and safety of other road users.

There is no element of theory testing and a commentary drive is not required.

More detail about the Cardington test is available from the DSA on 01234 744000 or at www.transportoffice.gov.uk/crt/drivertraining.

Institute of Advanced Motorists (IAM)

The IAM's advanced driving test has been operating since 1956 using Metropolitan Police principles of advanced driving.

You can take the test at various locations around the country. It lasts about 90 minutes and usually covers 30 to 40 miles on all types of road, including motorways if available.

The examiners are holders of the Police Advanced Drivers certificate and all have considerable experience in police driving methods.

IAM examiners are not looking for driving faults alone; they are trained to check for positive aspects of the driving as well as any negative points.

For more information, contact the IAM on 020 8996 9600 or at www.iam.org.uk.

Royal Society for the Prevention of Accidents (RoSPA)

The RoSPA advanced driving test normally lasts about one-and-a-quarter hours and is based on the principles in *Roadcraft* – the Police Driver's Manual.

RoSPA advanced tests are conducted at locations throughout the UK.

One unique feature of this particular test is that there is a grading system. At the end of the test the examiner discusses any points that have arisen and allocates a grade according to the overall driving performance of the candidate.

Application forms and further details about the test can be obtained from RoSPA on 0121 248 2000 or at www.rospa.co.uk.

DRIVING INSTRUCTOR QUALIFICATIONS

Several additional qualifications are available, each of which will help you to improve your skills and widen the scope of your normal everyday work, as well as adding to your CPD portfolio.

NVQ in driving instruction

NVQs are designed to meet the needs of today's businesses and can be targeted towards your requirements, especially for CPD.

The NVQ in driving instruction comprises several units that can be tailored to reflect the work of the individual. Each unit is made up of a number of occupational standards.

Details of courses in your area can be obtained from LearnDirect on 0800 101 901 or at www.learndirect.co.uk.

Diploma in Driving Instruction

The Diploma, which is awarded by the DIA (see page 219) in conjunction with Middlesex University, is an ideal way to add to your CPD.

Possession of the Diploma by an instructor enables the public to identify those instructors who have proved their professional competence. This not only benefits the individual instructor's business activities, but also adds value to the CPD portfolio.

The Diploma syllabus consists of five separate modules:

- Legal obligations and regulations.
- Management – practices and procedures.
- Vehicle maintenance and mechanical principles.
- Driving theory, skills and procedures.
- Teaching – practices and procedures.

The DIA arranges exam centres in various parts of the UK. Study materials for independent training are available from DIA.

To find out more about 'DipDI', contact the DIA on 0845 354 515, or at www.driving.org/professionalqualifications.

City & Guilds

The Certificate in Further Education (7407) qualifies you to teach part-time in further education.

Some of the skills involved in preparing for the qualification include:

- identifying and assessing learners' needs;
- planning the learning process;
- selecting and developing resources;
- providing learners with support;
- maintaining quality.

In general terms, the award is aimed at part-time teachers in FE and anyone who delivers vocational training to groups. It is, therefore, another useful addition to CPD.

For more details, contact City and Guilds on 0207 294 2800 or at www.cityandguilds.com/documents/ind-education-training/7407.

RoSPA National Diploma in Advanced Driving Instruction

The Diploma is mainly designed for instructors who provide training for candidates preparing for the RoSPA Advanced Driving Test (see page 214).

It is also relevant for anyone who wishes to develop their ability to train to an advanced level, both in-car and in-class.

The Diploma provides you with the core skills necessary to demonstrate advanced driving techniques and methods of instruction. It is, therefore, an appropriate qualification in relation to CPD.

Course content includes:

- effective classroom management techniques;
- teaching aids and presentation skills;
- facilitators and barriers to learning;
- instructional commentary on all types of road and environment;
- methods of providing remedial help and advice;
- monitoring the effectiveness of intervention;
- instructional ability;
- theory, practical and classroom exams.

For more detail, contact the Royal Society for the Prevention of Accidents (RoSPA) on 0121 248 2000 or at www.rospa.com/driver-training/courses.

Appendix I

Useful addresses

Driving Standards Agency (DSA)
The Axis Building
112 Upper Parliament Street
Nottingham NG1 6LP
Tel: 0115 936 6666
Web: www.dsa.gov.uk
www.direct.gov.uk/drivingtest
www.businesslink.gov.uk/transport

Customer service enquiries:
Tel: 0300 200 1122 (practical)
0300 200 1188 (theory)
Welsh line: 0300 200 1133
Fax: 0300 200 1177 (theory)
0300 200 1155 (practical)
Hearing-impaired customers:
(minicom): 0300 200 1144
e-mail: customer.services@dsa.gsi.gov.uk

ADI (Approved Driving Instructor) enquiries:
Tel: 0300 200 1122
Fax: 0300 200 1155
e-mail: adireg@dsa.gsi.gov.uk

DSA Training Centre and Learning Materials (Cardington):
Tel: 01234 744000

Driving and Vehicle Licensing Agency (DVLA)
Longview Road
Swansea SA6 7JL
Tel: 01792 782 341

Drivers' enquiries:
Tel: 0870 240 0009; Fax: 0870 240 1651
Hearing-impaired customers: 01792 766 366
e-mail: drivers.dvla@gtnet.gov.uk

Vehicle enquiries:
Tel: 0870 240 0010
Fax: 0870 850 1285
Hearing-impaired customers: 01792 766 426
e-mail: vehicles.dvla@gtnet.gov.uk

ADI consultative organizations

AA Driving School
3rd floor
St Patricks House
17 Penarth Road
Cardiff CF10 5ZA
Tel: 0800 328 8288
e-mail: driving@theaa.com
Web: www.AAdrivingschool.co.uk

Approved Driving Instructors National Joint Council (ADINJC)
General Secretary
16 Grosvenor Close
Lichfield
Staffordshire WS14 9SR
Tel: 01543 256578

e-mail: liasonofficer@adinjc.org.uk
Web: www.adinjc.com

British School of Motoring Limited (BSM)
RAC Building
2610 Quadrant
Aztec West Business Park
Bristol BS32 4TR
Tel: 08458 519579
Web: www.bsm.co.uk

Driving Instructors Association (DIA)
Safety House
Beddington Farm Road
Croydon
Surrey CR0 4XZ
Tel: 020 8665 5151
Or: 0845 345 5151
Fax: 020 8665 5565
e-mail: DIA@driving.org
Web: www.driving.org

Driving Instructors Democratic Union
(A branch of UNITE)
Chairman, DIDU
PO Box 165
Northallerton DL6 2WX
Tel: 0800 6226027
e-mail: info@didu.org.uk
Web: www.didu.org.uk

Driving Instructors Scottish Council (DISC)
4 Burnside Road
Uphall Broxburn
West Lothian EH52 5DE
Telephone: 01506 855455

e-mail: aeneas.disc@tiscali.co.uk
Web: www.d-i-s-c.org.uk

Motor Schools Association GB Ltd (MSA)
101 Wellington Road North
STOCKPORT
Cheshire SK4 2LP
Tel: 0161 429 9669
Fax: 0161 429 9779
e-mail: mail@msagb.co.uk
Web: www.msagb.co.uk

Training Aids and Services

DeskTop Driving Ltd
Unit 6
Gaugemaster Way
Ford
Arundel
West Sussex BN18 0RX
Tel: 01903 882299
Fax: 01903 885599
Web: www.desktopdriving.co.uk

Driving School Aids
Low La
Horsforth
West Yorks LS18 4DD
Tel: 0113 258 0688

Driving School Supplies
2–4 Tame Road
Witton
Birmingham B6 7DS
Tel: 0121 328 6226
Fax: 0121 327 1864
Web: www.d-ss.co.uk

He-Man Dual Controls Ltd
Cable Street
Southampton SO14 5AR
Tel: 023 8022 6952
Fax: 023 8033 0132
Web: www.he-mandualcontrols.co.uk

Porter Dual Controls
Impact Business Park
Greenford
Middlesex UB6 7JD
Tel: 020 8601 3566

RCM Marketing Ltd
20 Newtown Business Park
Albion Close
Poole
Dorset BH12 3LL
Tel: 01202 737999
Fax: 01202 735 909
Web: www.rcmmarketing.co.uk

SmartDriving
Ballinultha
Boyle
Co. Roscommon
Ireland
Web: www.smartdriving.co.uk

The Stationery Office (TSO)
PO Box 29
Norwich NR3 1GN
Tel: 0870 600 5522
Web: www.tsoshop.co.uk

Wholesale Book Supplies
18 High St
Bala
Gwynedd LL23 7AG
Tel: 0800 195 2208
Fax: 0800 195 2209
Web: www.wholesalebooks.co.uk

Motoring organizations

Automobile Association
Member administration contact centre
Lambert House
Stockport Road
Cheadle SK8 2DY
Tel: 0870 600 0371
Disability helpline: 0800 26 20 50
Fax: 0161 488 7544
Web: www.theaa.com

Royal Automobile Club
Customer services
Great Park Road
Bradley Stoke
Bristol BS32 4QN
Tel: 08705 722 722
Web: www.rac.co.uk

Business Contacts

British Franchise Association
Tel: 01865 379 892
Web: www.thebfa.org.uk
The governing body for franchising in the UK.

Useful Addresses

Business Eye (Wales)
Tel: 0845 796 9798
Web: www.businesseye.org.uk
Business advice service with centres across Wales.

Business Gateway (Scotland)
Tel: 0845 609 6611
Web: www.bgateway.com
Advice and information for start-up and existing businesses in Scotland.

Business Link
Tel: 0845 600 9006
Web: www.businesslink.gov.uk
Advice and information from the UK Government for new and existing businesses.

Career loans
Tel: 0800 585 505
Tel: 0800 585 505
Web: www.lifelonglearning.co.uk
Loans for initial vocational training.

Companies House
Tel: 01222 380801
Web: www.companieshouse.gov.uk
Advice on statutory obligations for company directors.

Department for Business, Innovation and Skills (BIS)
Tel: 020 7215 5000
www.bis.gov.uk
Advice on financing and raising capital.

Enterprise Agencies
Tel: 01234 831623
Web: www.nfea.com
Advice on setting up and running a business.

Federation of Small Businesses
Tel: 01253 336000
Web: www.fsb.org.uk
Promotes and protects the interests of the self-employed and small businesses.

Health and Safety Executive (HSE)
Tel: 0845 345 0055
Web: www.hse.gov.uk
Information and advice on health and safety in the workplace.

HM Revenue and Customs (HMRC)
Tel: 0845 010 9000
Newly self-employed helpline: 0845 915 4515
Self-employed contact centre: 0845 915 4655
NI Registration helpline: 0845 915 7006
Self-assessment helpline: 0845 900 0444
Web: www.hmrc.gov.uk
Local tax office: www.hmrc.gov.uk/local/individuals
Information on tax, allowances, National Insurance and VAT.

LearnDirect
Tel: 0800 101 901
Web: www.learndirect.co.uk
Information on all levels of skills learning.

Nominet UK
Tel: 01865 332244
Web: www.nominet.org.uk
Registration of domain names.

Small Business
Web: www.smallbusiness.co.uk
A comprehensive website offering advice on all aspects of starting up and running a small business.

Small Firms Enterprise Development Initiative
Web: www.sfedi.co.uk
Range of services for small businesses.

Start your own business
Tel: 023 8074 0400
Web: www.syob.co.uk
Free local guide providing useful local information to anyone thinking of setting up on their own.

Young People's Learning Agency
Tel: 0845 337 2000
Web: www.ypla.gov.uk
Setting standards for skills in the workplace.

Banks

(For advice and business start-up packs)

Alliance and Leicester
Business Banking
Tel: 0800 587 0800
Web: www.alliance-leicestercommercialbank.co.uk

Bank of Scotland and Halifax
Business
Tel: 0845 950 0505
Web: www.bankofscotland.co.uk/business

Barclays Bank
Small Business Banking
Tel: 024 76 6944242
Web: www.barclays.co.uk

HSBC Bank
Business Unit
Tel: 08457 43 44 45
Web: www.banking.hsbc.co.uk

Lloyds TSB Bank
Small Business Advice
Tel: 08000 560 056
Web: www.smallbusiness.co.uk

NatWest Bank
Business Banking
Tel: 020 7920 5555
Web: www.natwest.com

Royal Bank of Scotland
Small Business
Tel: 0131 523 4069
Web: www.royalbankscot.co.uk

Appendix 2

Further reading

Driving

Your Road to Becoming an Approved Driving Instructor (ADI 14)
Driving Standards Agency (DSA)
£5.00

The Official DSA Guide to Driving – the essential skills
DSA/The Stationery Office
£12.99
ISBN 0 11 552817 2

The Official Guide to Learning to Drive
DSA/The Stationery Office
£7.99
ISBN 0 11 552608 0

The Official DSA Theory Test for Car Drivers and the Highway Code
DSA/The Stationery Office
£11.99
ISBN 0 11 552 839 3

Know Your Traffic Signs
DSA/The Stationery Office
£4.99
ISBN 0 11 552855 5

The Highway Code
DSA/The Stationery Office
£1.99
ISBN 978 0 11 552698 5

The LGV Learner Driver's Guide
John Miller
Kogan Page
£14.99
ISBN 978 0 7494 3790 9

Instruction

The Driving Instructor's Handbook (16th edn)
John Miller and Margaret Stacey
Kogan Page
£19.99
ISBN 978 0 7494 5539 2

Practical Teaching Skills for Driving Instructors (7th edn)
John Miller and Margaret Stacey
Kogan Page
£18.99
ISBN 978 0 7494 4953 7

Instructional Techniques and Practice for Driving Instructors
L Walklin
Stanley Thornes
£18.50
ISBN 0 7487 1631 9

Helping Learners to Practise – the Official DSA Guide
DSA/The Stationery Office
£7.99
ISBN 0 11 552611 0

Coaching for Performance
John Whitmore
Nicholas Brealey Publishing
£12.99
ISBN 1 85788 303 9

Business

Starting a Business from Home
Colin Barrow
Kogan Page
£12.99
ISBN 978 0 7494 5194 3

Working for Yourself
Jonathan Reuvid
Kogan Page
£12.99
ISBN 978 0 7494 5058 8

Start up and Run Your Own Business
Jonathan Reuvid
Kogan Page
£12.99
ISBN 978 0 7494 5061 8

Law for the Small Business
Patricia Clayton
Kogan Page
£15.99
ISBN 0 7494 4149 6

How to Choose a Franchise
Iain Murray
Kogan Page
£9.99
ISBN 0 7494 4195 X

Appendix 3

Information links

Most of the information about motoring, learning to drive and driving instructor matters can now be found on the Directgov website – www.direct.gov.uk.

Some of the more useful links:

direct.gov.uk/motoring
Information, forms and leaflets on driver licensing, learner drivers, road safety and vehicles.

direct.gov.uk/drivingtest
Online bookings for car and motorcycle tests.

direct.gov.uk/motoringnearest
Addresses for your nearest driving test centre, theory tests, official register of driving instructor training (ORDIT).

direct.gov.uk/motoring forms
Forms for driving tests, licences, vehicle registration and taxation.

direct.gov.uk/motoring leaflets
Leaflets relating to driving tests, licences, vehicle registration and taxation.

direct.gov.uk/motoringonline
Interactive tools for transactions, services, forms and leaflets.

direct.gov.uk/arrivealive
Information about the 'Arrive Alive' programme.

direct.gov.uk/cbt
Compulsory Basic Training for motorcyclists.

direct.gov.uk/driversrecord
Preparing for the driving test – the driver's record.

direct.gov.uk/driving
Driving licences.

direct.gov.uk/drivingtestfees
Driving test fees.

direct.gov.uk/ecosafedriving
Eco-friendly and safe driving.

direct.gov.uk/highwaycode
The Highway Code online.

direct.gov.uk/learnerdrivers
direct.gov.uk/learning2driveInformation for learner drivers.

direct.gov.uk/motoringpublications
The Stationery Office online bookshop for DSA publications.

direct.gov.uk/passplus
Information about PassPlus.

direct.gov.uk/theorytest
Theory test information.

direct.gov.uk/roadsafety
General road safety information.

Index

NB: page numbers in *italic* indicate figures or tables

AA, the   10
  AA driving school   64
accidents   190–91
  legal definition   190
  reporting an accident   191
ADI exams
  application forms   28
  course material   48
    Driving Test report form   48
    Helping Learners to Practice – the Official DSA Guide   48, 173
    Highway Code   13, 19, 21, 43, 48, 152, 154, 203
    Practical Teaching Skills for Driving Instructors   2, 29, 39, 43, 48, 52, 136, 137, 207
    The Driving Instructor's Handbook   1–2, 3, 9, 29, 31, 38, 39, 48, 52, 136, 137, 182
    The Official DSA Guide to Driving – the Essential Skills   13, 48, 154, 167
    The Official DSA Guide to Hazard Perception   48, 154
    The Official Guide to Learning to Drive   48, 154
  criminal record disclosure (CRD)   28
  driving ability test   32–36
    controls   34–35
    eyesight test   32
    judgement and planning   35–36
    number of attempts allowed   36
    routes   33
    syllabus   33–34
    vehicle safety questions   32–33
  instructional ability   36–39
    exam tips   38
    number of attempts allowed   38
    pass rate   49
    structure   36–37
  reading material   29
  theory test   9, 29–31, *30*
    hazard perception   31
    pass marks   29, 31
  training courses   45–47
  training programme, choosing a   44–45
  training providers   47, 48–51
ADI, becoming a
  benefits, of being an instructor   15–16
  check test   2, 28, 40–43, 69
    check list   42–43
    core competencies   40
    grading system   41–42
    instructional techniques   41
    instructor characteristics   41
  competition   10
  cost of training   9
  costs   16–17
  customers   10
  driving skills   17–26
    braking   18–19
    defensive driving   21–24
    eco-friendly driving   18, 24–26, 36
    lane selection   21
    signalling   19–20
    steering   20–21
  earning power   9, 15–16
  exams   *see* ADI exams
  female-to-male ratio   10
  franchising
    advantages of   7–8
    fees and costs   16
  instructor training   43

Index 233

Official Register for Driving Instructor Training (ORDIT)   43–44
national driving schools, working with   7
personal qualities   11
    anticipation   12–13
    communication   14–15
    concentration   12
    confidence   13
    hazard awareness   15
    knowledge   13–14
    patience   13
qualifying as an ADI   27–28
responsibilities   12
trainee licence   39
working hours   11, 16
ADT   97
advanced driving courses   181
    Cardington driving test   212–13
    Institute of Advanced Motorists (IAM)   181, 213
    Royal Society for the Prevention of Accidents (RoSPA)   181, 213–14
    see also Pass Plus
Advertising Standards Authority   144
anti-lock braking system (ABS)   185
Approved Driving Instructors National Joint Council (ADI NJC)   209–10

Blackberry   105
bookkeeping   120–22
    bookkeeping software   122
    cash book   121
    purchases record   121
    sales record   121
British School of Motoring (BSM)   10
    franchising   65–66
Business Link   87
    grants and support directory   88
    legal structure of businesses advice   61
    start-up organizer   87
business plan, making a   54–55, 75–80
    and applying for business funding   88, 91–92
    business plan checklist   76
    figures to include   78
    lesson pricing   80
    structure of the plan   78–79
    SWOT analysis   77–78

uses for   76
caravans and trailers   201
Cardington driving test   212–13
cash flow   79
Central Motor Auctions   97
check test   2, 28, 40–43, 69
    check list   42–43
    core competencies   40
    grading system   41–42
    instructional techniques   41
    instructor characteristics   41
child seats and restraints   *189*, 189–90
    second-hand child seats   190
coaching   51–52
GROW   52
Coaching for Performance   52
Compulsory Basic Training (CBT)   149
continuing professional development (CPD)   6, 206–16
    advanced driving courses
        Cardington driving test   212–13
        Institute of Advanced Motorists (IAM)   213
        Royal Society for the Prevention of Accidents (RoSPA)   213–14
    definition of   206
    driving instructor qualifications
        City and Guilds Certificate in Further Education   215
        Diploma in Driving Instruction   214–15
        NVQ in driving instruction   214
        Royal Society for the Prevention of Accidents (RoSPA) National Diploma in Advanced Driving Instruction   216
    for lorry drivers   207
    and marketing your business   208
    professional associations
        Approved Driving Instructors National Joint Council (ADI NJC)   209–10
        Driving Instructors Association (DIA)   210
        local associations   212–13
        Motor Schools Association (MSA)   211
    record keeping   208
    skills to cover   207
    ways of training   209
criminal record disclosure (CRD)   28

234 Index

customer care 131–40
   advertising 144
   car, state of the 138
   checklist 139–40
   code of practice 142, 144
   complaints, handling 140
   conversation 139
   customer documentation 143
   customer expectations 131
   customer loyalty, winning 131
   customer service, basic rules of 141–42
   dress code 138
   Driver's Record, maintaining 133–34, 137
   enquiries 134–35
      dealing with 132
      following up 132, 36
   feedback, getting 133
   first lesson 136–37
   personal conduct 142–43
   personal contact 139
   personal recommendations 132
   private practice 137–38
   smoking 138
   terms of business 143
   test applications 144
   training schedule 137

Data Protection Act 103
Department for Transport (DfT) 145, 206
Department of Business, Innovation and Skills (BIS) 87, 88
disabilities, learner drivers with 147, 175–76
drink/driving 187–88
   alcohol limits 187
   penalties 188
Driver and Vehicle Licensing Agency (DVLA) 145
   applying for a licence 147–48, 179
   notifying the DVLA 146, 150
Driver Certificate of Competence 204
driver number 146
Driver's Record 133–34, 137, 167, 174
Driving Instructor 210
Driving Instructors Association (DIA) 210
Driving Instructors Scottish Council (DISC) 212
Driving Instructors' Group 209–10

driving licences
   application forms 147–48
      Post Office Premium Service 148, 150
   eyesight 146
   fees 150, 180
   full licence, getting a 179
   history of 145
   large vehicles 180–81
   licence categories 146, 180
   minimum age, for driving 146–47
      and disabled drivers 147
      in other European countries 147, 182
   motorcycles and mopeds 148–50
      Compulsory Basic Training (CBT) 149
      licence categories 150
   penalty points 181
   New Driver Act 181–82
   photocard licences 145, 146
   provisional licences 146, 148
   renewals 146, 150, 180
   replacements 150
   trailers 180
   vocational licences 151
Driving magazine 210
Driving School Pro 137
Driving Standards Agency (DSA) 4
   instructional ability exam tips 38
   instructor starter pack 11, 17, 28
   Official Register for Driving Instructor Training (ORDIT) 43–44
   Pass Plus starter pack 199
   review of driver training 4–6
driving tests, for examiners *see* ADI exams
driving tests, for pupils
   practical test
      applying 156–57
      cancellations 161
      Certificate of Competence to Drive 161
      Driving Test Report 160, 61
      duration 160
      examiners 158
      eyesight test 158–59
      failing the test 161
      fee 157
      passing the test 160–61
      safety checks 159
      syllabus 157–58

test centres   157
test format   158–60
theory test   151–56
    cancellations   155
    failing the test   155
    fee   152
    hazard perception   153
    mock tests   154
    pass mark   153, 154
    passing the test   155
    special needs   154–55
    syllabus   152–53
    test centres   152, 156
    trainer booking   151

eco-friendly driving   18, 24–26, 36, 191–93
    definition of   191
    tips   25–26, 191–92
Edinburgh Driving Assessment Service   176
Enterprise Finance Guarantee (EFG)   87
eyesight
    in the ADI exams   32
    of pupils   146, 158–59

Farlam, John   52
Federation of Small Businesses   109
fleet driver training   201–02
    qualifying   202
franchising   62–68
    AA driving school   64
    advantages of   7–8, 63
    British School of Motoring (BSM)   65–66
    checklist   66–67
    disadvantages of   63
    fees and costs   16
fuel efficiency   *see* eco-friendly driving

Goodwood Motor Circuit   1
Google   128

health and safety
    Health and Safety at Work Act   106, 107
    Health and Safety Executive   107
    risk assessment   107
    and smoking   107
Helping Learners to Practice – the Official DSA Guide   48, 173

Highway Code   13, 19, 21, 43, 48, 152, 154, 203
holidays   118–19
    contact in your absence   119

Institute of Advanced Motorists (IAM)   181, 213
instructor, becoming a   *see* ADI, becoming a
instructors, employing   122
insurance   70, 95, 108–12, 172
    accident, giving details after a   191
    breakdown cover   98
    and business expenses   115
    business insurance   109
    in your business plan   78
    and disqualification for drink/driving   188
    and the Driving Instructors Association (DIA)   210
    and franchising   16, 64
    and health and safety   107
    and instruction in the customer's own vehicle   200
    insurance checklist   112
    motor insurance   109–10
    and the Motor Schools Association (MSA)   211
    National Insurance   8, 53, 59, 68, 69, 70, 74, 117–18
    and bookkeeping   120
    and employing other instructors   122
    and Pass Plus   173, 177, 178, *179*, 197, 199
    personal insurances
        employer's liability insurance   111–12
        health insurance   111
        life insurance   111
        office contents   111
        professional indemnity   112
        public liability insurance   100, 112
    and pre-driver training   165, 166–67
    and running costs   17
    and tax allowances   117
    and using cars for practice   171
    and using your home as an office   101
intensive courses   168–70, 195–96
    pass rate   169
International Driving Permit   182

236 Index

iPhone   105

Know your Traffic Signs   152, 154

large vehicles   180–81
LDC   66
Learner Driver Centre   10
legal business structures
   franchising   *see main entry*
   limited company   61
   partnership   60
   sole trader   58–60
lessons
   cost of   175
   frequency of   168
   number needed   174–75
   structuring   167
LGV training   203–05
   compulsory training   204
   licence categories   203
   voluntary register   205
licence categories   146, 180
Local Enterprise Agencies (LEAs)   88
location, of your business   79

marketing   79, 123–30, 132
   advertising   125–26
   business cards   124
   business directories   125
   checklist   130
   discounts, offering   133
   e-mail marketing   129
   honesty in advertising   133, 144
   leaflet drops   124
   local press   124, 125
   marketing budget   124
   press releases   129–30
   pricing of lessons   125
   promotional literature   133
   website, setting up a
      checklist   129
      pay-per-click advertising   128
      search engine optimization (SEO)   127–28
      website content   128–29
minibuses   200
minimum age, for driving   146–47
   and disabled drivers   147
   in other European countries   147, 182
Mobility Advice & Vehicle Information Service (MAVIS)   175

Motor Schools Association (MSA)   69, 211
motorcycles and mopeds   148–50
   Compulsory Basic Training (CBT)   149
   licence categories   150
motorway driving   186–87
   and Pass Plus   186
MSA Newslink   211

National Health Service (NHS)   110, 111
National Insurance   8, 53, 59, 68, 69, 70, 74, 117–18
   and bookkeeping   120
   and employing other instructors   122
New Driver Act   181–82
Nokia   105

Official Register for Driving Instructor Training (ORDIT)   43–44

Palm   105
Pass Plus   176–79, 181, 196–99
   benefits of Pass Plus   177
   cost of   177
   fees   197
   and insurance   173, 177, 178, 197, 199
      insurance companies   *179*
   and marketing   124
   and motorway driving   176, 186, 187
   registering as a Pass Plus instructor   178, 199
   structure   177–78
   syllabus   197–99
   what it is   176
   when to take Pass Plus   178, 199
   who runs it   176
penalty points   181
   New Driver Act   181–82
Pension Service   72
pensions   72–73, 119–20
   and National Insurance   117
   pension planning   72–73
photocard licences   145, 146
Post Office Premium Service   148, 150
Practical Teaching Skills for Driving Instructors   2, 29, 39, 43, 48, 52, 136, 137, 207
practical test   *see* ADI exams; driving tests, for pupils

Index

pre-driver training   162–67, 195
   advantages of   163
   age limit   165
   cost of   164
   definition of   162–63
   disadvantages of   164–65
   and driving licences   165
   with friends and family   166–67
   getting involved   164
   group instruction   166
   and insurance   165, 166–67
   syllabus   163
   theory classes   163
private practice, getting   170–71, 173
   and insurance   171, 172
   supervising driver   171
   with friends and family   170, 173
Professional and Career Development Loan (PCDL)   90
provisional licences   146, 148

Queen Elizabeth's Foundation Mobility Centre   175

RED Driving School   66
Regional Development Agencies (RDAs)   88
risk assessment   79
Roadcraft   213
Royal Society for the Prevention of Accidents (RoSPA)
   Advanced Driving Test   181, 213–14
   National Diploma in Advanced Driving Instruction   216

SatNav   98
seatbelts   188–89
   child restraints   189, *189*
   exemptions   189
   legal situation   188
self employed, becoming   53–73
   advantages   53
   business plan, making a   54–55
   business skills
      administration   71
      banking   74
      bookkeeping   71–72
      finance   73
      financing assets   73–74
      management and planning   70–71
      National Insurance   74
      pension planning   72–73

      tax   72
      VAT   73
   cancellations   58
   disadvantages   54, 68–69
   and holidays   55
   legal business structures
      franchising   *see main entry*
      limited company   61
      partnership   60
      sole trader   58–60
   legal obligations   68
   research and planning   54
   SWOT analysis, doing a   56–57, 77
   time management   57–58
skidpan training   186
Skype   105
speed limits   182–83, *183*
Stacey, Nigel and Margaret   1, 2
starting up your business   75–99
   advisory services   87
   budgets and cash flow   81–87
      cash flow forecast, making a   81, *82–84*, 85
      profit and loss projections, making a   85, *86*
   business plan, making a   54–55, 75–80
      and applying for business funding   88, 91–92
      business plan checklist   76
      figures to include   78
      lesson pricing   80
      structure of the plan   78–79
      SWOT analysis   77–78
      uses for   76
   car, getting and equipping your   92–99
      automatic cars   96–97
      buying your car   93
      choosing your car   94–97
      depreciation   94–95
      equipment and extras   97–99
      fuel costs   96
      insurance costs   95
      maintenance   96
      manual cars   96
      new cars   96
      renting or leasing your car   94
      replacement costs   95
      size of car   92
      used cars   96
      and VAT   94

warranty 96
where to buy your car 97
loans, grants and finance 88–92
  applying for business funding 88, 91
  bank loans 89
  borrowing from friends and
    family 90–91
  choosing a bank 89
  credit card, using a 90
  Enterprise Finance Guarantee
    (EFG) 87
  grants 88–89
  information to provide 88
  leasing / renting 91
  overdraft, using a 89–90
  Professional and Career
    Development Loan (PCDL) 90
  sources of funding 88
  using a business advisor 89
start-up checklist 80
stopping distances *184*, 184–86
  and anti-lock braking systems
    (ABS) 185
  braking distance 184
  on wet roads 184
  separation distance 185
  and skidpans 186
  thinking distance 184
SWOT analysis
  in your business plan 77–78, 79
  for your business idea 56–57, 77

tax 112–17
  expenses, claiming tax
    against 115–17
  HM Revenue and Customs,
    informing 113
  income tax year 53, 113
  keeping documents 114
  key tax dates 114–15
  payment schedule 113, 114
  self-assessment 72, 113–14
taxi driver assessments 202–03
*The Driving Instructor's
  Handbook* 1–2, 3, 9, 29, 31, 38,
  39, 48, 52, 136, 137, 182
*The Official DSA Complete Theory Test
  Kit* 154
*The Official DSA Guide to Driving – the
  Essential Skills* 13, 48, 154, 167
*The Official DSA Guide to Hazard
  Perception* 48, 154

*The Official Guide to Learning to
  Drive* 48, 154
*The Official Theory Test for Car
  Drivers* 154
theory test *see* ADI exams; driving
  tests, for pupils
Thomsons 10
trailers 180
trainee licence 39

using your home as an office 70, 100–02
  and business rates 100
  and Capital Gains Tax 100, 102
  and council tax 101
  equipment 102–06
    computer 103–05
    computer accessories 102, 105
    e-mail address 106
    internet phone 105
    mobile phone 106
    netbooks 105
    printer 102
    SmartPhone 105
    software 102
    stationery 102
    telephone 106
    wireless 105
  and health and safety 100
  insurance 101
  mortgage or landlord's
    permission 101
  neighbours 101
  planning permission 71, 101

VAT
  and administration 71
  registering for VAT 58, 73, 108
vocational driver training 200
vocational licences 151

website, setting up a
  checklist 129
  pay-per-click advertising 128
  search engine optimization
    (SEO) 127–28
  website content 128–29
Whitmore, John 52

Yahoo! 128
Yellow Pages 10, 127
Young People's Learning Agency
  (YPLA) 90